THE
SOUND
OF
LIGHT

LEONARD SWEET
LISA SAMSON

THE
SOUND
OF
LIGHT

*Speaking Words of
Hope and Comfort
to Those Who Are Suffering*

WHITAKER
HOUSE

Scripture taken from the *Holy Bible: Easy-to-Read Version* (ERV), International Edition © 2013, 2016 by Bible League International and used by permission. Scripture quotations marked (ESV) are taken from *The Holy Bible, English Standard Version*, © 2016, 2001, 2000, 1995 by Crossway Bibles, a division of Good News Publishers. Used by permission. All rights reserved.

THE SOUND OF LIGHT
Speaking Words of Hope and Comfort to Those Who Are Suffering

ISBN: 979-8-88769-282-1
eBook ISBN: 979-8-88769-283-8
Printed in the United States of America
© 2024 by Leonard Sweet and Lisa Samson

Whitaker House
1030 Hunt Valley Circle
New Kensington, PA 15068
www.whitakerhouse.com

Library of Congress Control Number: 2024911304

1 2 3 4 5 6 7 8 9 10 11 ᴡʜ 31 30 29 28 27 26 25 24

CONTENTS

BOOK 2: WORDS OF HOPE TO READ ALOUD WITH THOSE IN CRITICAL CONDITION

NOTE TO YOU WHO
READ ALOUD

You are about to embark on a journey of love not only with the Beloved One who is before you but with the One who loves you too. Each entry is written to be read aloud by you, as you. Own the *I*, the *me*, the *my*, the *us*, the *we*, the *our*, and the *ours*. And as you inhabit yourself as the giver of these words, you will receive the love of God and all the blessing and care it provides to you too.

Feel free to note thoughts, feelings, dates, and conversations in the pages of this book as you journey through these readings.

Whether you read aloud in a room next to your loved one, over the phone, or leave a reading as a voicemail to be played over and over, know you are loving your Beloved.

Be blessed in this act of caring and compassion, Beloved. You are as equally loved in every moment as the One you now serve.

Be loved, Beloved. Be loved.

BOOK 1:

WORDS OF GRACE
TO READ ALOUD WITH THOSE
AT LIFE'S END

Be loved, Beloved. Be loved.

For every child of God on the cusp of life's greatest adventure.

1

THE LIGHT THAT NEVER LEFT HAS COME

The sun rose today all over the earth. The clouds could not stop it from coming and lighting up our blue marble planet, which turns, turns, turns.

The sun is always present, as you know. It never takes a rest. It shines warm, burning bright even as our planet revolves for one more day. Each revolution reveals the care and concern of the One who made the sun, the earth, and all we now dwell in.

The day arrived yet again, dragging you and me along with it. Every day is both no different than yesterday, yet a totally new day dissimilar from every other day we've ever lived. It is our lot as humans to find that "still point of the turning world." And in that stillness, we can wonder why we exist. Why are we here?

We can be assured of one thing, one reason we exist: each new day brings the opportunity to be—to be love and to be loved.

So, Dear Friend of God, the God who loves all of us, be love and be loved today. Be loved by the One who made you and me—the One who deems you lovable and worth loving.

This love is just like light from the sun. Its warmth falls upon your heart straight from the heart of God. Listen to this song that echoes in the chambers of your heart, where God abides:

"I have loved you with an everlasting love" (Jeremiah 31:3 ESV).

You are beloved, unconditionally loved by God. You can never be loved too much. "True Light" is the *Logos* Light that loves you out of hurting and hiding. "True Light" is the only light you can trust with your life and the life to come.

Be loved, Beloved. Be loved today. By God, by me, by others. If you can do but that—let Love love you—you will have surpassed a conqueror's dream or a king's ransom. The love of God received is the peace of God restored. It is freely given to all. To you. To me. Endlessly to be received, beyond measure, beyond words.

Be loved, Beloved. Be loved.

2

EVERY DAY ARRIVES
WITH NEW LIFE

Beloved, yet another day has begun. The world continues, each minute of the hour, each minute point on the planet, all loved by the One who made them, and made you. New beginnings have been happening your entire life and will keep happening.

All the babies being born today, tomorrow, and the next day are no exception. Every newborn baby is evidence of God's endless dream of streaming love. Today more of us will appear just as you did the day you were born. Each human birth is a God-dream come true. You are a God-dream come to life, a divine nativity. Each human is made to love and be loved by the Creator.

You are loved right now just as much as any little one that sticks their head out today. You might ask, "How can I even compare to innocent newborn life?" With humans, this is impossible, but with God, it is totally possible.

Time isn't something to which God is chained. In the realm of the Divine Eternal, what is fifty, sixty, seventy, eighty years compared to a second, a minute, an hour, a day? Barely a breath. Hardly a beat of the heart. To the timeless heart of God, you are still a beloved newborn.

So, Child of God, you are still here. We rejoice in your continued presence. Though this fleeting chapter of time shall close, you are still that babe in arms, held closely to the heart of the One who made you.

Your eyes are gazed into by the eyes of your loving Parent, who not only created you but also made stars to light your night and one to rule your day. Watch all of it together, you and God, even if to do so you must recall the velvet skies in the vast space of your mind.

As you now put last things first, rest in the arms of the One who delights in all that was made, including the newborn babies, including you and me. God will never let us go. The One who helped us find our way here will be the One who helps us find our way back. One day, in the amazing grace of God—one day, soon and very soon—you can say, "I once was blind, but now I see," and by that same amazing grace, "Was bound, but now I'm free."

God will never let you go, Beloved Child. You are forever cared for, you are held, you are loved with an everlasting love.

You have this moment to be loved by God. Receive that love. It's what brings God joy and you peace.

Be loved, Beloved. Be loved.

3

BROKEN ROADS
STILL LEAD HOME

While it has been said that "all roads lead to Rome," it is even more true that "all roads lead to home."

Even broken ones, Beloved.

No human has walked an unbroken road: illness, drama, and trauma seem to take jackhammers to the avenues of our lives. The unrelenting rains of change, delivering loss and sorrow, sweep across our paths. Pieces of our hearts rush away as the flood washes out bridges and tears down trusses. Despite what our outward appearances say, we know the truth: roadblocks rear before us, downed trees surround us, swollen creeks and stark winds pummel us.

Whatever your road has disposed, whatever errant paths or twisted lanes you've wandered on, please know your road has led you here today. From this day forward, God will lead you home in grace. This fork in your road need not be yet another detour but it can be the first step onto the peaceful path you've been searching for all your life.

God's path that exists beyond time and space, the sunrise boulevard of blessedness, is the path where you are cared for and cherished every single step, and every single moment. Child of God, the beautiful truth is, your road home has always existed in God's deep love for you. It is beneath you even now.

Trust the road. God's love is never-ending, ever present, your whenever destiny. God calls you home and helps you make it home. God has prepared a home for you and for me. We all can call home. That's called prayer. But one day God will call us home. That's called paradise.

Does the broken road matter now if the destination has always been you're home in God's arms? Do the slips and slides, the potholes and pitfalls, the wanderings and wonderings make a difference to the One who carried you then, the One who carries you now?

Indeed, not.

Rest assured of this: mercy, grace, and favor are yours now, tomorrow, and forevermore.

Keep your eyes on home, the finishing school of life. Home is where one chapter of your story ends, and another begins. Home is where you are viewed, valued, and understood as the beautiful creation you are to the One who made you.

God has collected our tears in a bottle on the mantle at home, where all we have ever done is weighed not against what is perfect, but by what we have suffered. When we are brought home, we need not be ashamed, for our Divine Parent says, "See here, this. I know, I know, I know. Rest now, Child. Rest."

God knows all. God knows. God knows. God knows the way home. God will lead you perfectly home.

There is nothing to fear. You have only to—fly home. To fly home is to fly home to God, where you will be loved, Beloved. Be loved.

4

LOVE THAT FEELS LIKE LOVE

Among those who speak and hear these words, not all of us have experienced an idyllic childhood to which our minds might return for safe harbor. But we all know what love feels like.

God is love. So any time in your life you have felt love, given love, or glimpsed love, you have experienced a speck of God. This all-consuming love that bounces around the world, slips in, covers up, stares down, holds forth, crosses under, feeds back, touches on, mends with, stands for, and chips away all walls that separate—this is the very same Love that made you, that made me, that made all of us.

Here are a few truths common to all.

Love thought you were a very good idea, Beloved. Love still does and wants you to feel as loved today as you truly are. This is love's story.

Love feels like the warmth of the sun. Light arrives simply because it does, not because it wants anything in return. It's free and here to stay, and in its glow and flow you have always lived.

Love feels like the air in currents, circulating through the branches, rushing down the valleys and over plains, filling your lungs with life. Needy we are of its grace. Its favor abounds in every breath you and I take. All the world is invited, all of us say yes. You and I included.

Love feels like the rush of a river, the sound of water over rocks, the veins of life feeding the ground in which grows all that we need, all that you have ever needed to face the sun's light for one more day.

Love feels like the moist, fertile earth in which a seed burrows, sprouting at the appointed time, then held in the arms of the soil. It feeds us, our growth, and our blossoming, into that which the One who made us intended.

Love feels like the person who not only cares for you but cares about you.

Love feels like one who comes at your darkest hours, sits with you amidst confusion and pain.

Love accepts your madness as something other than who you are, rejoicing when the beautiful and good creation you truly are surfaces once again.

Love laughs with you and sings over you in all your moments of joy.

Love feels like God. Because God is love, and God's story is a love story.

God is love, Beloved. Loving you, loving me, now having loved us always, and loving all eternally. In light, in air, in water, in soil, by day, by night.

Be loved, Beloved. Be loved.

5

ABIDING LOVE NEVER LEAVES

Love abides, and we abide in love. The abiding love of God for all creation, including you, including me, cannot go away or else it ceases to abide. But God is love, and God is everywhere. So God's love comes to us in abundance and in abidance. Love abides with you and with me, always. Even now, and forever.

God made you, Dear Friend, not just to receive divine love in fits and starts. Sure, there are times in your life when you have felt it more strongly than others. But God made us to live in that love, to abide completely in the love that abides with us always.

Abide in God today, Beloved. In the presence of the abiding One, that love will reveal itself to you in more ways than you know or might imagine. Your present circumstances cannot thwart even one way in which God can become Presence.

With you now abides the One who made you, and not just you, but me, and all that God brought into being. Everything that exists is a manifestation and declaration of God's love.

With you abides the One who orchestrates the song of the stars.

With you abides the One who floods the earth with light.

With you abides the One who covers the earth with a blanket of night to give rest, to refresh, to restore, to start anew a new day. Even now the One is regenerating your inmost being, readying you for your journey further into God's light.

Like a mother who will not leave the side of her ailing child, God abides with you now, holding your hand, whispering assurances that you are cared for, singing a lullaby as you are carried into the light of the setting sun.

Abide, Beloved, abide. Be still in one peace, and know all that is necessary is to be—to be as you are, a child of God. You walk the bridge that spans the yawning chasm between this world and the next. As you step on that bridge, feel the steely strength of God's love beneath you, an impregnable love that transcends time and scaffolds space.

Be held in the arms of grace, and step after step, be loved, Beloved. Be loved.

6

COME IN, BELOVED, YOU ARE ALWAYS WELCOMED

Imagine a night so cold and dark, each star is seen yet more perfectly in all its twinkling, sparkling radiance. Imagine a mountain so high and wide, its peak looks out upon the world below. The climb is steep and exhausting, but in the distance a warm light glows. You feel its welcome, a beam of invitation, drawing you in. It feels like home.

We all have been brought into homes like that a time or two. A kind, curious soul inhabits the interior, and we are welcomed with a hearty greeting, a warm meal, and a saved place by the hearth. "Tell me about yourself," your host asks—eager to know you, excited to bring more of you into the nurturing acceptance that welcomed you when you walked across the threshold.

That's God's house. That's God's abiding place. The One who made you invites you to sit down and talk about it all. Do you know that about God? God is fascinated by you, enthralled to hear your story, ready to experience you in the perfect home, on the perfect mountain, looking over the clear cold night and the light of stars around you. God is raring to love you, perfectly love you. Is that not the way it has always been?

God yearns to sit with you in truth, Beloved. Cast all your cares away and hand them over to the One who binds up your wounds and bind up in arms of love all the things others did to you that wouldn't slip out of your fingers. God will listen to each one and help you lay all of that aside and forgive that which the One who loves all already has. Leave that heavy backpack in the mudroom so that all grievance that held you back will be washed away. Give God every piece of clothing you couldn't throw out, every piece that didn't fit, every item that constricted you and cut off your freedom. Let that heavy load go; there's no good reason not to.

God sits with you even now. Take this opportunity to tell the One who made you about all the things you love about being human. Tell the One who loves you all that you have been grateful for in your daily living, even those wonderful, once-in-a-lifetime gifts that came your way. Tell the One who delights in you about each blessing and feel your heart swell with gratitude: "Yes, I saw. Yes, I received. Yes, it made me so happy. Thank you, God, for that."

There is no wearing out your welcome! Come, one and all; come, you and me. No cold shoulders will turn when you enter this haven. No silent treatments will be given. Your suitcase is never packed up and waiting for you to vacate the premises. God is in residence for the long haul and in relationship for life eternal. You are invited right now to sit down and bare your heart.

God is eager for you to be lavished in divine love, for that reception, my Friend, is what often has been missing. But at that beautiful house of warm woods, colorful stone, and a bubbling pot of heart-warming soup, you cannot help but receive the love. Because that love is all there is.

In the meantime, Beloved, let's sit together at the table, you and me. Let's experience the perfect reception in this moment as we listen to the song of love that is our Maker's joy. You are loved. All are loved.

Pull up a chair right now and luxuriate in the warmth, the peace, the sustaining love that is your God.

Be loved, Beloved. Be loved.

7

THE TREASURE HAS ALWAYS BEEN RIGHT HERE

Every child loves drawing maps with broken lines leading to that magical, mysterious X that "marks the spot." Finding buried treasure strikes a chord in all of us. Oh, that life could be that easy.

Perhaps you've been searching for treasure all your life. Most do, maybe we all do, and in ways unique to each. We draw a life map with the pursuits of possessions, power, pleasure, position, and prizes of all kinds. Even great meaning along our path feels more like food for the hunt.

I have a secret to tell you. The treasure has been with you all along. The treasure is with you now, Beloved. The treasure is God's pleasure. The treasure is buried deep inside you: God's abiding presence.

Open the box that springs alive at your touch. It has been waiting for you to pick it up. Fasten your weary gaze upon the treasure inside. You will find grace for all the times you made mistakes. You will find forgiveness for all the times you hurt yourself or others. You will find mercy for anything else that you may be struggling to let go of right now.

There isn't anything inside you that cannot be healed—fixed and then handed back to you perfectly restored, as a treasure from the One who made you. It is the same One who longs to give you all the treasures of the world to come.

Dig your hands into the mounds of gold, precious rubies, diamonds, and sapphires. Don't forget the pearl of greatest price, your own relationship with God. See the soft glint of your relinquishment to the holy as the treasure of abiding love slips through God's fingers and down into your inmost being.

Dear Friend, all that's necessary from you now is to open your hands and heart to receive that love. It's all that's left to do. Like a treasure buried deep in the earth compounds interest by gathering more and more value, God's love will flame within you, igniting all that once lay cold and forgotten. God loves all of you. You, Beloved, are God's treasure, unearthed and open to the glory of the One who made you.

Be treasured, Beloved. Beyond measure. Beyond time. It is God's good pleasure for you to be loved, Beloved. Be loved.

8

THERE'S A PARTY ZONE
WITHIN YOU

You might find this hard to believe, and I don't blame you if you do. But there's a party going on inside you right now. In truth, there's a party going on inside me too, inside everybody. But where you are gives you the distinct advantage of feeling the party more keenly than many of us.

God is throwing this party and has been since the dawn of time. When God made you, rejoicing began. It has never stopped. What confetti of joy erupted when you first walked, talked, giggled, and gave your first toy to another child!

The angels get in on it too. The heavens rejoice every time someone says "Yes" to the love God has for them. I suspect they rejoice as well every time we forgive others and accept the love and goodness they extend our way.

What if the party is getting ready to go into full swing? What if you can hear its music faintly already? Perhaps you can imagine those who will be there to welcome you across the threshold. The party feels like joy, like love, like the celebration of a homecoming or family reunion with all your favorites—favorite foods and favorite people.

How can you know it will be like that? Because God knows what you love best and created you to love that way. No cookie-cutter people, no cookie-cutter homecomings.

You are welcomed, you know. God loves you no matter what. The unconditional nature of the love of God is exactly that. All those jokes about St. Peter at the gates need not apply. God is there, open armed and loud voiced, speaking your name and saying, "Come in,

Child." God is there, celebrating your arrival and announcing to all, "My Beloved is home!"

What God has always known, now you know. You have never left the light of God's love, the home of God's heart. You know right where you are. You're already there, and so am I.

What a gift to be received!

Heaven rejoices and sings and the One who made you leads the band.

Be loved, Beloved. Be loved.

9

THE SHIP OF SIGHS WE ALL HAVE SAILED

Let's slip into that safe place inside our minds where pictures are formed and stories are fashioned. That is where portraits and voices are folded like stacks of fabric, like pallets of wood and metal. Be free to build the Ship of Sighs that you have been sailing on all life. The river of life, with its ebbing and flowing, groans and growls, sighs and whispers, is the only motion sustaining your emotions, the only waters on which you have plunged or stalled.

Around us, the sea roars, and the sun casts harsh rays. You can hear it howl. You can feel the heat. Monsters await like the Hydra of happenstance, hissing, squalling, and calling above the din. The ship still sails today for us all. But the din grows more quiet as the years go on. The screams become sighs, the sighs become memories, the nightmares fade in the face of the glorious Presence that had been saying "I love you" all along. In the din, in the sighs, in the nightmares, and in the fading of dreams, God's "I love you" never ceases.

Let's rechristen the "Ship of Sighs" as the "Ship of Sight and Light." The Master sailor is now at the helm, calling out perfect orders.

When the wind is at its peak for the ship's structure, when all sails are unfurled and billowed to their fullness, when the rigging is taut, and there is a oneness of wind, climate, and craft, the boat begins to hydroplane. The ship starts levitating over the waves and wind. You know a vessel is maxed out to its limits in the wind and levitating over the water when you hear the hum. The sailing vessel hovers and hums in its sweetest spot and at its fastest speed.

Do you feel it, Child of God? Do you hear the hum? The hum of holiness? The vibrations of oneness? Do you feel the lightness of being? Let your vessel realize the full sailing in the winds. Let your body feel its quickening above the waters. Air all around you. Light inside you. Let go. No need to pull in your sails. It's time to fly upon the wind of Love. It's time to be loved, Beloved. Be loved.

10

THERE'S ONE MESSAGE
IN EVERY BOTTLE

Beloved, bottles constantly bob on the surface in the sea of life. From the multitude of possibilities, we make our selections. One bottle among the many we pick again and again. In one bottle, the kiss of lovers, your first good one leading the way. In another bottle, all the flowers you would ever feast your eyes upon. Most likely, when opened, a dandelion springs forth, or perhaps a buttercup.

The bottles of childhood came in great profusion, bottles with labels like "cloud formations," "rushing rivers," "things with fur," and "things that fly."

Foods that taste like they were made from the heart.

Winds come in all kinds, from boats, a fan on your face, to the bluster of a sudden storm.

Anything soft and smooth against your skin.

Anything cooling your parched summer throat.

Loving touches.

There are bottles of music that make you sad and ones that fill your heart with every "Yes" you might cry out. There are bottled words of gentle concern from loving relatives, teachers, friends, or the person who saw you crying in the parking lot. There are words of praise and congratulations. There are loving sounds in every register your spirit has ever recorded.

The bottles are with you now. Each one, however different in color, size, and shape, ultimately has a singular message—a message from the One who made you. Each folded-up letter says, "I love you."

Gather your bottles and toast the joys. I will gather mine, and let us open them all afresh, here with each other. From the bottom of our hearts, let us toast the bottled blessings of life: old wine to drink, old wood to burn, old books to read, and old friends to enjoy.

Love letters, Dear Friend, to all that is, was, and evermore shall be. Love letters telling you to be loved, Beloved. Be loved.

11

THE PERFECTION OF ALL GOD MADE RECOGNIZES ITSELF

Family reunions can be some of life's greatest delights—and disasters. One contrarian uncle, one pushy aunt—a handful of disapproving, disgruntled, disillusioned relatives can taint the waters. But they don't spoil the joy or the pleasure of those genuinely happy to be there in the presence of close relations, of unspoken connections, some rooted generations deep. These are the people we know, in all their ways, for better and worse, for all our lives. Or all of theirs.

Add time and distance between gatherings, and you experience the joy of recognition. Of course, we don't need a reunion to experience that satisfaction. It's in the voice of a friend you haven't talked with in years. It's in an email, a wedding announcement, a Christmas card, a squeeze on the shoulder when you haven't received one in a very long time.

The sorrow caused by the loss of these experiences is one of life's greatest hurts. But a great recognizing is coming for each one of us. Dear Friend, "re-cognize" literally means to re-know. Those who await, who have gone on, will be re-known by you in perfection. And you, Beloved, in all your God-created goodness, will be recognized by them in theirs. You will be re-known in the full beauty of God's design. Maybe even without the windedness, weathering, and time-touched cracks and creases. Not to mention all those barnacles on the skin that maddeningly appear out of nowhere.

This is a family reunion like no other. Everyone's siblings are equally loved and uniquely yoked in perfect love and wholeness. When the circuits are completed, the electricity really flows—the electrifying, everlasting love of God. There are no tears, only unsurpassable joy.

Love abides there in completion, as it does here. But there, you will recognize it in yourself and everyone you meet or meet with again.

Love abides here now in fullness, too, folding and enfolding you. God is always to be found in all places, all times, and all circumstances. No up or down, no in or out. Perfectly present when we pay attention to the Perfect Presence.

Let the reunion and the recognition begin by receiving the love that is always here, the love of the One who made you and will never let you go. In that be loved, Beloved. Be loved.

12

THE RIVER WILL CARRY
YOU GENTLY

The river of life takes us with it no matter how hard we swim against the current. How much easier would it be if only we bobbed like a cork or slid like a leaf? But we brace ourselves against change. We slam against rocks and get ensnared in fallen trees. Isn't it wonderful news that resistance doesn't reroute the river that leads onward in the fullness of time?

Why we humans tend to fight against change, or the future, is easy to explain but hard to justify. What lies ahead is always a mystery. But God is always ahead of us and at the front of all mysteries. How hard we try to control outcomes by controlling ourselves and others. So it goes, and even so, God is still there with you—in, with, and under the river, rocks, trees, sun, sky, in every bit of it. In all of it, God loves you, really loves you.

Yes, you are coming to a bend in the pathway, the bend we all must take sooner or later. But the river is nothing to fear, even as the greatest mystery lies ahead. There is no skeletal boatman at the helm. There is really no crossing at all. The river continues, and its name is Eternal Love.

There is a toll, however. The toll consists of all your pain, anguish, and sorrows. We can pay the toll at any time throughout our lives.

That toll includes all you thought was true but isn't, all you wanted that cannot make you happy, all the wild expectations you had of yourself and others, all that you attained only to find it doesn't bring you lasting peace, the peace that passes all understanding.

Now peace is here and around the bend, Beloved! Sound the bells, blow the trumpets, strike the drums! Peace is here. Listen.

Hear God singing the loudest, a song of love that is the river that you and I are traveling right now. Receive the flow of the Boatmaster, whose voice will accompany you home. Receive God's accompanying love and care for you, me, and all God made. Let God take it from here. Trust and be loved, Beloved. Be loved.

13

THE DEEPEST ROOM WITHIN YOUR HEART IS FILLED WITH LOVE ALONE

There's an invitation extended to you now. It doesn't require anything but your willingness to imagine yourself with the One who made you. This One lives within you in the deepest place you abide, the inside place you share. In the innermost room, you will find the One who loves you most, the One who helps when you earnestly cry out, and the One who guides when you let God lead instead of inviting God along for the ride.

Far down in the deepest room lies a compassion far beyond human understanding. The One who collects our tears in a bottle, the One who knows all things, still loves us and always will abide there.

The deepest room may have felt shuttered off by pride, guilt, shame, anger, disappointment, or despair. The wounds of others can make it hard to open. But none of that has been too much for the One who knows our wounds, who has been there with us all along. That locked door to our deepest room has been blown open by a holiness that cannot be caged or changed, not by anything you have ever thought or done, not even by wounds you have suffered or injuries you have inflicted.

The One who bears our wounds longs to heal you, hold you, and grace you with mercy so deep and wide, so fresh and free, it is beyond your current imagining—mine too.

Come in, Beloved. Enter into the space where a perfect God welcomes an imperfect you perfectly. Your Creator sees who you were made to be and stops right there. Who can measure such mercy or meter such compassion? The One who made you, the One who made all things. The One who gets you.

Be loved, Beloved. Be loved.

14

THE AIR THAT MOVES UPHOLDS YOUR WINGS

Watching a large hawk catch the wind and play with it is thrilling. It hovers and soars at times, peeling off at others. As we witness sweeping dips and silent circles, we feel the instinctual joy of a creature relishing what the Creator meant for it to experience, utilizing their own design to its fullness.

Remember wishing you could do that as a child? But the air feels far different to us. It is fragile to the utmost, sundered by anything captive to Earth's gravity. We plummet through it, the very stuff we breathe to stay alive. For air to become that kind of force, a being needs to rise above it.

With God as your wind, your breath, your moving force, however, you need not fear a plummet, Beloved. God is already all around you, in you, with you to the uttermost. Even now, Beloved. Especially now.

Receive the Love that made you. Allow that Love to float you in its streams of grace. God's mercy endures from everlasting to everlasting. God loves you, Dear One, not because God looks the other way but because God's gaze can't be removed from you. You are held in the gaze of a grand affection that gives, forgives, and gives again. The One who is with you loves you just as you were created—as God's child. When you have a hard time remembering that, it is God's affection for you that remembers on your behalf.

"I am here," the One who made you whispers in the deepest chamber of your heart. The breezes of love can come forth from that love, that place of union that can be forgotten but not expunged.

Open the chamber door, Beloved. Receive love's holy breath into your inmost being, feel its grace lifting you, and soar.

God is with you. God is here upholding you.

It's time to soar and be loved, Beloved. Be loved.

15

BY SOME MIRACLE OF GRACE, WE LEAD EACH OTHER HOME

In many ways, part of being human entails leading each other to God. From the cradle, many of us heard about God in stories, songs, and sacred passages. We were taken to services and festivals, feasts and celebrations, laments and blessings. We write about these things too. Did you read books like this one written with an implement held in human hands that related an experience of God? We love each other enough to share our journey, hoping that some of it can be put to good use.

We have subtle and overt conversations about God, religion, faith, and how to relate to each other in light of the Spirit. When we view one another in love, accepting the inherent beauty of God's creation, the path becomes brighter. We can walk it in wholeness and joy. I see you, Child of God. I invite you to see me too.

Consider this amazement: God is gracious enough to speak to us as we are, and from our experiences together. Think about how creation coalesces around us in the heavens and the earth. Think about the way our skin feels when it touches skin. Think about the music we make together. Think about anything good we do, anything beautiful we create, and any truth that God reveals to us. God's grace is there to the brimming and overflowing, and we take each other one step closer to home.

Remember today your fellow humans who were most influential in leading you back to God—walking with you, crying with you, rejoicing with you, and respecting you enough to tell you the truth in love. They picked up the phone after midnight and came to get you for whatever reason—silly or grave. Sandwiches made, pieces of cake coaxed down, a coat for covering, gloves for protection, and a sparkled thing for no reason but the spark of sparkle.

God has been talking to you this whole time, Beloved! Since you first made your presence known in your newborn cry, God has heard, God has witnessed, and God has loved.

God has loved you!

Receive these moments of profusion anew and pleasure in the recall of those who love and have loved you. It was God's will from before time that you should luxuriate in love. Let God love you in plain sight. Sunbathe in it today, as this has been God's plan all along.

Abide in that love that doesn't mind telling you and reminding you repeatedly from the lips and hands of others. Love is unstoppable, like a rushing, swollen stream eager to jump the banks in joy, always whole but never quite the same.

Let us experience the love anew, Dear Friend, and be loved, Beloved. Be loved.

16

THE SKY DECLARES THE GLORY OF GOD, AND THAT GLORY IS LOVE

The sky might be the most beautiful thing we humans get to witness. It changes throughout the day as clouds tumble in separately or slide in like a wave ready to deposit rain to replenish the earth's arteries and veins. Everyone gasps at the splendor of sunsets, but don't forget the mystery of mists or the glamor of clouds.

The sky's atmosphere is mostly made up of oxygen and nitrogen, with a little argon thrown in to make things interesting. The Earth, with ever-changing concentrations of dust and moisture, dirt and water, courts the atmosphere before our eyes. What happens after the intercourse of the earth and sky is beyond our control.

But one baby is always born from the congress of heaven and earth: color. A light display of depth and variance blazes forth as we spin toward and away from the sun. Our every movement angles our view of the light, intensifying the scene as our perception of what's above us changes according to the Earth's direction.

Further yet, we spin. Sometimes we can see the moonlight brace cartwheeling clouds, silvered by night. Our trusty satellite always echoes the illumination of our star, so there is also a singing with all the stars.

Darkness, Dear Friend, is a myth we have fabricated. We like to think that if we cannot see, God cannot either. But with God, darkness is as light (see Psalm 139:12). The light of God's vision and love are like the sky that is never truly without illumination. No matter what the clouds tell you or the insides of boxes declare, the love of the

One who made you is always in full view: glorious, gratis, and beyond your control and mine. Isn't that marvelous?

Just like the heavens light up, God lights up and displays divine love before you. God will do so even now. Rest and receive without telling God how to do it. You don't have to, and you never have. Let the mystery shine; let the glory be. The One who displays divine handiwork has created the firmament of love for you, me, and all the heavenly hosts. The light of God's love is neither controlled nor extinguished; all of it is in favor of God's children—you, me, all of us.

Be loved, Beloved. Be loved.

17

INSIDE HOLDS WONDERS YOU CANNOT SEE WITH AVERTED GAZE

The life of God—the life that God desires to live with, in, and through you—is like a grab bag, handed to you at the beginning of your life. Do you remember playing carnival games? There are two kinds of carnival games (besides the rigged ones): games of skill and games of chance. Target shooting was a game of skill. Picking up the "lucky duck" was a game of chance. Maybe you played both for that mysterious bag in a cupboard of prizes.

You have to give up all command and control with a mystery bag. A treasure trove is always a tour de force of relinquishing and risking. You live with the possibility that you might have been better served at the mole-whacking game around the corner. But taking a chance is worth it. The feeling of laying it on the line for a mystery brings an incomparable high and a thrill up the spine worth the possible loss.

This time, the bags are filled with treasure far greater than King Solomon's treasures! The bag has a humble covering because it can only be that way. The take-a-chance grab bag signifies our life journey. We must accept that all God made is good—including all your limitations, all my limitations, all of you, all of me. In that acceptance, you come to know the One who made you is good. Reach out and grab that simple, humble little bag, Beloved. Open that treasure chest.

A treasure island of love rests inside!

Love that knows you even better than you know yourself!

Love that values you far more than you could think to value yourself!

Love that will shepherd you beside still waters (see Psalm 23) and to the highlands with confidence when the floodwaters rise.

Love that creates beauty.

Love that makes the heart hammer.

Love that makes whole and binds wounds, inner and outer. Love that heals our hearts.

Love that can bring about the well-being of one without sacrificing the well-being of all.

Love you can trust.

Gaze upon love in its natural grab bag presentation. Reach inside, jump inside, dance inside the everlasting love—the love that will never let you go, beloved Child of God.

Take hold of the treasure found inside humility and trust. Receive the riches of a humble yet lavish grace, never given to be admired or seen, only imparted in love and implanted in your spirit to be loved, Beloved. Be loved.

18

STILL ENOUGH TO HEAR THE TENDER VOICE OF GOD

Your innermost being is the most untroubled part of you. Why? It is joined to God in the Creator's very image within you. Minds are troubled, spirits get down, and hearts are broken. But there is a place of quiet rest within you, God's all-loves-excelling place.

Just for this moment, still your heart, Beloved. Lift your spirit to God. Calm your mind. Be still in the peace of the eternal being you truly are. Be held in the arms of the Prince of Peace. In the stillness of God's presence, peace flows like a river, and joy alights upon every speck of light that warms you. The comfort that stillness provides is the comfort of a child who knows their parent is on their side no matter what, sick or well, victorious or crushed.

Enter the stillness that is the union of your will with the will of God for you. Welcome the serenity and insight of the Divine Presence accompanying you no matter the next step.

Be still enough to listen for that love that comes softly—like whispered affections in the ear or the gentle touch of a mother's hand on the fevered brow of her child.

Quiet, Beloved. Do you hear the stillness? Can you listen for the love that says you are found worthy by the very nature of your creation, to be cared for and ushered forth? Can you hear the wooing of God who is taking your hand even now, and even now?

God is here, my Friend. God is with you in stillness. This is especially evident when you allow the Divine Presence to be as it wishes, like a mother's tenderness, the protectiveness of a father, and the companionship of a sister or brother. The friend that never leaves you or forsakes you. God is all that and more than any of us can speak of as we make din with our tongues, and God tells us be loved, Beloved. Be loved.

19

THE LOVE OF GOD IS
LIKE THE RAIN

The wider the field, the more raindrops can soak into its soil. Your life is no different, Beloved, nor is mine. Perhaps you were taught life was like a cistern into which the rain fell and was collected into bins, basins, and buckets.

But God's rain, God's love, falls far beyond the boundaries we have set for it. There are no boundaries to the love of the One who made you, the One who loves you, the One who is with you.

Open the gates of your heart, Beloved. Your field is ripe to receive the gentle rains of God's overflowing love for you right now. It is patient, kind, and enduring. It is not easily angered and keeps no record of wrongs. It always protects, always provides, always trusts, always hopes. Love never fails. (See 1 Corinthians 13:4–8.) You can trust it with your life. You can trust it will do all it promises and intends. You can trust you will be cared for in its embrace today.

Simply receive and let God do the rest. God will, Beloved! The One who made you, who made me, will do this for all of God's children who spread their arms, raise their weary and wounded hearts, and say "Yes" to God even as God says a never-ending "Yes" to all of creation. There are no exceptions, Beloved. Not a one. Just lift your hands and say...

"Yes, my Maker. Yes, and yes."

The rain of God's love is steady upon the Earth, greening fields, swelling creeks, and settling dust. In the shadow of the rain, crops grow and feed the earth; animals walk, fly, and swim in their creaturely existence; and trees abound, manufacturing oxygen and shading us from noonday heat.

This is and always has been for you, Dear Friend, for me, for all of us. Let love be like rain on your heart after a drought; let it be a draft of drink in the desert.

Be loved, Beloved. Be loved.

20

HIDE AND SEEK IS NOT GOD'S GAME

There's no more need to play hide and seek with the One who made you, Child of God. All games are not real, but this one is especially false. Many have described themselves as seekers. Many have said they have a hide-and-seek relationship with God. But a lie that comes under righteous cover is still a lie. The truth is this: God is the seeker; we are the hiders. Who can hide from God? Who can find God if God does not wish to be found?

Besides, we've really been playing peekaboo with God all along. Like little children, we have covered our eyes and been mistaken about God's absence. But God abides with you, me, and all of us. God is the One who is everywhere—always.

Like a good, kind, loving parent, God has been right before you, playing your game of "I'll Pretend You're Not There" with you. So God hides in plain sight: in a cold drink, a warm blanket, the whisper of nature when it speaks its breathy tones, a friend's treating you to lunch, munchies, anything they know you'll find filling and fulfilling. God is in those new experiences that bring a joyfulness you didn't know before. The One who walks with you shod your feet, lights your day, lifts your head, and never averts a loving gaze. No matter how you are otherwise—how tightly you shut your eyes or how firmly you plug your ears—God looks at you and speaks to you regardless.

Says God:
I am with you in all your days and nights.
Sound of Light
I feel your pain.
I see your sorrow.

I love you as you are.

You and I share a home not made by human hands, an everlasting abode, infinite and capable of being anywhere you and I are.

Keep your eyes open, your ears clear, your heart receptive, and know you have never been parted from the One who loves you from everlasting—and will love you, me, and all of us—to everlasting.

Be loved, Beloved. Be loved.

21

GOD WILL CARRY ANY LOAD WE PLACE INTO THE DIVINE HANDS

God is like a friend with a pickup truck on a moving day. Not only does the One who made you show up to help, but God will also help you with the appliances, the piano, and any other heavy item you cannot carry yourself.

What's more, God is a cheerful helper, Beloved. The One who loves you pulls up with a tray of drinks and a smile. Humans have given God a bad rap since time out of mind. No, the One who is always with you is NOT a grievance-filled grump who says, "You got yourself into this mess, you can get yourself out of it," or words like, "Why should I care when you keep making the same mistakes over and over again?"

Yes, God is fully aware of our missteps, mistakes, and misdeeds. God knows our refusal to see the beauty and worthiness in ourselves and others exactly as God created us. But there is no more gracious helper in existence than God. God remembers our humanity. God recognizes our frailty. With a grace so lavish and a heart hooked on goodness and love, God understands our weakness. God forgives our stubborn attachments to cages and confinements we locked ourselves in. Cages like refusing to forgive, taking for granted life's blessings, or cutting ourselves off from what life is truly about: love and connection. When we flog ourselves for these failures and labor under the lash of limitations, whether forced upon us or embraced by us, God shows us how to eliminate these heavy burdens we were never meant to carry.

God instructs you to just drop it all. Right now. Forgive yourself. Forgive those who have wronged you, both the living and those who have gone before. Remember the good of others, the good you have done, and be blessed in your abounding gratitude. It's time to turn over to the One who knows all the weighty boxes you have carried for so long. Be assured that God will carry even the good you can no longer hold onto. All you have to do is say, "Take it. It's Yours."

You are God's Child. Isn't that incredible? You are cared for and loved. Those you care for and love are also held in the arms of God. Let God have them all.

God will honor your trust. No burden is too heavy, and no box is too small. All that's left to do is receive the love of the One who loves you, the One who wants to carry your load, Dear Friend.

Be loved, Beloved. Be loved.

22

DEEP BENEATH YOU THE ROOTS
OF LOVE GROW

There have been some storms, haven't there, Beloved? The world we see, plowed, planted, populated, peopled, is the world of red skies: winds and wild cards, black swans, and white elephants. No one ever prepares us for how life twists and turns, tumbles, and rumbles its way forward. It is as if we must try not to believe life is so because if we admit it, things will get worse, not better.

How not so with God!

You've been through a lot. You've watched with your eyes, felt with your skin, tasted with your tongue, breathed in (for better or for worse) with your nose. You've listened with your ears to the sensual symphony of life above ground. We judge our security and stability by the world we experience on the surface. We succumb to the cartwheeling allures and caterwauling cries of power and glory, jewels to be sought, bought, earned, and stored.

But we cannot forget when we felt most safe—the rocking of the cradle by the family that accepted us, or the hugging of friends who came along when the family didn't, who loved us exactly for who were.

Exactly who you are, Beloved, is someone not fully living in the shining and glimmering world of the seen but more and more abiding in the soil of the unseen, a place teeming with heat, life, and creativity as the decayed is received and reworked by some of the tiniest creatures on earth. You are rooting in the invisible. You are germinating in the unseen love of the One who made you. Sublime beauty is the invisible made visible. Your essence is rooted and routed, reaching out countless fingers in every direction into the nourishing soil of the One who never leaves or forsakes you.

Rest in your roots. Luxuriate in the deep part of you, the underground quiet places where you're so close it's hard to tell where you end and God begins. You exist there, you know. Roots grow deep so that plants can flourish in the light. All you have to do is receive God's love for you. The One who loves all creation will hold you close. There's no need to fear the unknown because that is the way to the heights and heaven.

Be loved, Beloved. Be loved.

23

WHEN THE WIND POWERS
THE BOAT

There's a big difference between a sailboat experience on the open water and a powerboat experience.

When the breeze picks up and fills the sails, it is a world of difference from when the motor kicks in and pushes the craft forward. The little chug, sometimes beginning with a blue puff of smoke, propels the boat along of its own accord. It will only go as fast as the motor allows.

But the wind is another story! The wind requires the boat to adjust to it. When the skillful sailor sets the sails just right, the speed and agility of the boat as it moves through the water are awe-inspiring and life-giving. Even the wind on our faces feels more thrilling when it comes from canvas sails, not fuel tanks.

The breath of the One who created you will take over the propulsion of your life at any time you ask. God takes our will very seriously. Maybe it's time to say, "Yes, God, hoist the sails, set the course, take me where You will. Pilot me."

"Yes, God" is like cutting off the gas-heaving motor and hoisting the sails. God will help you adjust them along the way so that the wind might carry you more effortlessly and efficiently.

It's never too late to say "Yes" to God's powering and piloting. Even now, God is ready to breathe holy breaths of love into your being so that you might continue your journey. Sail upon the waters of the One who loves you with the breath of the One who is with you. God will sail your boat now.

God will take care of you.

Kick back, lean forward, and glide. Trust. Receive the love of God for you. The One who loves you will guide your craft to a safe harbor. In that harbor, as now, is the everlasting life found in the One in whom you live and move and have your being.

And when you reach the shore?

Home. The home is prepared for you! The ship that God sails always delivers safely into the harbor. When we say "Yes" to God, we're really saying "Yes" to a ship running the way it was meant to run and to a dream destination fully furnished for us by our Maker and Creator.

It's an advancement...

to goodness without transaction,

to love without a breaking point,

to light and warmth unending.

It's where you will be known and know, fully as you are. Can you see the lighthouse? God is at the helm. God will guide you through anything between you and the front door. You'll be welcomed home by the One who rules the waves, your loving Parent.

It's hard to imagine, but don't let that stop you, Friend! Imagine with all the zest and zeal inside you. Do not feel anything is too magnificent for God, because it is not. Eye hasn't seen, nor ear heard, the wonderful things God has prepared for you. (See 1 Corinthians 2:9.)

See safe harbor, sailor, and be loved, Beloved. Be loved.

24

GOD LOVES TO SHOW UP
IN DISGUISE

Do you have a friend who doesn't dig at you or wound you repeatedly but welcomes you regardless of what you bring to the friendship? If yes, you have experienced God in human disguise as a relationship. For some of us, it might be hard to imagine such a person. For others, a face comes to mind. I hope it's that way for you.

Do you have a place in life that you go to physically or mentally when you need to be alone with your thoughts? Maybe a mountain hideaway, a view of an ocean, a place by a river or lake, a park bench, a path in a forest, or a field where clouds pass over? If yes, you have experienced God in disguise as a place to abide.

Do you have memories of an unexpected check when the power bill came due, a gift card to throw a party for a loved one, gas money, a basket of food, a place to stay, and a garment to wear? If yes, you have experienced God in disguise as provision and providence.

God meets you, me, and every single one of us in many ways. But we spend most of our lives not recognizing it. We may even fool ourselves into thinking that what we pay for deserves no gratitude. "I earned it," we say. But unlike humans who skulk off after someone fails to acknowledge them repeatedly, God sticks around. God might even find you in other disguises.

Do you remember someone who just came to sit with you, love you, and hear you? If yes, you have experienced God as a presence. Do you have a healthcare professional who really cares and attends to your needs, from giving you water, smiling when you're discouraged, or tending to a complicated surgical procedure? If yes, you have experienced God as a helper and healer. God always heals. Sometimes, death is the final healing act. But God always heals.

In all these ways, all these people, Beloved, God shows up, loving you and telling you that you are known, celebrated, and loved.

See God in all the lovers and helpers.

Let God love you in all the ways God is doing even now. Let God love you in new ways, unforeseen and unimaginable by human minds. In all amazing and emerging ways, be loved, Beloved. Be loved.

25

"SANCTUARY!"

For many centuries, the cry of "Sanctuary!" fell from the trembling lips of those hiding in churches. Kings would not overrun the inner sanctum of a church or a cathedral when looking for a wanted person, a political enemy, or someone on the run from danger.

"If God wants that trouble, let God have it!" perhaps they thought. Or maybe, in moments of compassion, they pardoned a person to God's care and a life of service since they were so desperate to exile in church.

For me, for you, for all of us, God says, "Come in! Beloved Child, come in!" Sanctuary is the embrace of the One who loves you. Sanctuary is being surrounded with arms so strong you feel God's heart beat with joy and burst with understanding. The hearts of you and of the One who made you beat together and pulse in unison, "I am here!"

Like a frightened child raising their arms to a parent asking for a pick up, you will be lifted, scooped right up into the abiding presence of God. Even now. Like the sanctuary of old, what you've done, what I've done, doesn't matter there. When you raise your arms to be received by God, you let go of all the rights you thought you had that only brought you pain.

Be lifted, Dear Friend.

Be received, Child of God.

Be loved, Beloved.

And please know you are held in the Everlasting Arms. Does a parent forget their child?

Not this Parent.

Death isn't anything to be afraid of. This world and its trials and mysteries sometimes feel like a bad dream. But instead of an unending existence of these fearful scenarios, God has planned so much more for us. Leaving this world behind is like waking up from a nightmare and finding yourself safely tucked in your good Parent's arms, resting next to the heart of the One who loves you. Nothing to fear. The trials have ended. And you are home.

Rest, receive, and let the One who is with you now carry you, in perfect timing, to the sanctuary of the home you never truly left, the home we call God, the home we where are invited to be loved, Beloved. Be loved.

26

THE LOOKING GLASS THAT LOOKS BACK

Picture a mirror in your mind's eye. Perhaps you're standing in front of a bathroom sink. Maybe you're looking at yourself in the full-length mirror on the back of your bedroom door. Or you might be walking up to the glass doors of an office building.

We've spent enough time in front of mirrors. For the most part, what we see is an actual reflection of our physical form. Whether we like it or not, whether we appreciate it or take it for granted, we know what we look like. But there's a looking glass that you and I might gaze into for a more accurate reflection. What we see inside that mirror is not what we're used to seeing. It's our image as God sees us.

God sees you far differently than you see yourself, Dear Friend. The One who made you sees you as you were created to be. When God was done creating your form, God stepped back, took a deep breath of pleasure, and said, "This is good. This is true. This is beautiful."

Since the day all was formed, nothing about you, not one atom, is new. You are a miracle of space, time, and design, a knockout masterpiece from the Maestro Composer of life.

We all are.

God sees you, Beloved, as a thriving piece of all that is loved and sustained. But even more profound, God loves you. You have been known this whole time, and in that mirror is an unveiling of God's divine image. When God views your image, God sees the reflected glory of who you are. You are created to shine in this world and all eternity as a singular ray of the divine glory as God's perfectly created child.

God sees the beauty created by the One who loves you and finds what God made as perfect as ever. God did make it.

How is this possible?

God knows the end from the beginning. God knows where you're headed. You don't see a trade-in when you look at yourself in the mirror of the future. You see a trade up to life anew. You fully recognize who you truly are, God's offspring. It's hard to imagine that mirror. But you, me, all of us, will someday look into it. Concur with your Creator and say, "It is good." The Creator who is always telling us to be loved, Beloved. Be loved.

27

ALWAYS NEW, YET ALWAYS TRUE, THE LOVE OF GOD FOR YOU

New love announces its arrival. At first glance, you see your own reflection in the eyes of another. True love is seen in the shine of "I adore you" and in the sparkle of "I think you're wonderful." Pure love is found in the unsullied space where no one has yet wronged the other. No one has yet fallen short. No one has yet failed to live up to another's expectations. Pure love might be one of the most wondrous things about being human. The highest form of love, however, is when new, true, and pure love combine and combust in forgiving love. All human love needs grace granted and pardon offered—no matter how full our hearts are for our beloved.

But God.

God looks upon us with that shine no matter what. Yes, even when we go wayward or willful and do or say things we wish we hadn't, God is the love that always stays when we stray. God says, "I forgive you. Of course we're okay."

God is the love you can call when you spaced out and sideswiped the guardrail. God's first words are, "You're okay. That's what matters most to me." God is the love that already knows your absentmindedness. Your Creator never needs to hammer the nail home at the end of pointed words.

God is the love that hugs you when you're sweaty and smelly. God says, "I love every part of you. What's a little perspiration?"

God is the love that likes to make you an amazing sandwich for a midnight snack when you're overcome with sorrow. God is the love that sits with you while you eat it and says, "I'm here any time you need me."

God is the love that fetches the toilet paper when you find yourself stranded in the bathroom.

God is the love that brings your lunch to you when you've forgotten it on the counter.

God is the love that doesn't give a heavy, dramatic sigh when you leave the porch light on—again. God just turns off the porch light and climbs into bed beside you.

God is the love of small actions and everyday rescues.

This is the One who made you.

This is the One who loves you.

This is the One who never left you.

In all the small ways, God has loved you, is loving you, and will continue to love you.

In all ways be loved, Beloved. Be loved.

28

THE TENDER GREENHOUSE
PLANT IS PERFECT

Some deem the mighty oak and towering redwood superior to other beautiful plants in the garden. Really? Is the bristlecone pine less impressive than the hummingbird orchid? Both are beautiful in their own right. Both are created to be just as they are, visible unveilings of the invisible. God has placed them perfectly.

In colder climes, we cultivate tropical plants in greenhouses. But a greenhouse doesn't negate their created wonder or cast a spell of inadequacy upon their existence. No. We value them and desire them to thrive, no matter whether they're in their native habitat or not.

Life takes all of us, you and me, to a place where the freezing rains and thrashing winds are no longer sufferable or habitable. That's when God sweeps open the greenhouse door and welcomes us with "love divine, all loves excelling." It is a place of tending and mending until the day the door opens to reveal that spring has arrived. Perhaps you felt that in your life at times. You were taken aside and restored and refreshed. Maybe a friend invited you to be with them, or a movie gave you hope. Perhaps a book transported you to a reality where you realized life could be so much more. This wellspring arrives in more ways than the human mind can conceive.

Friend, these were just glimpses of an eternal spring of God's love in all its fullness. This spring awaits your recognition and release. The door opens at the slightest press of your palm. It welcomes you, fragile as you may feel, into the place that has been prepared for you—the place that is perfect for you. God best defines this place as *"Where I am you may be"* (John 14:3 ESV). God's presence is the perfect place of perfect peace. It is here always, and yet it is coming.

Yes, that prepared place is what is coming, Dear Friend. Simply let God love you as you are—here, in this place, in this time. Allow the people surrounding and supporting you to hold you up.

Step into spring, Beloved. Trust the love. Don't try to make yourself perfect. Trust God to set you in the right place, like a Master Gardener setting His most valued specimen in the paragon of settings, where God is perfectly capable of placing you. It's on God now when you say yes to God's love.

Step into the eternal spring of God's unchanging, abiding love.

Be loved, Beloved. Be loved.

29

THE STICK-BY-YOUR-SIDE, NO-MATTER-WHAT FRIEND

It is more than a little ironic that we have to tell God to get in the car.

But we all know this is true. We all know when we've kicked God out.

At least we think that's what we've done.

But, Friend, when you ask God to ride shotgun with you and don't kick God to the curb, the One who is with you always will be with you for the long ride.

The trip to that significant other's will end up breaking your heart.

The 2:00 a.m. ride to the gas station for that beer, those cigarettes, and the king-sized candy bar.

The ride to that dare—the resulting ride to the ER.

The ride home when you lost your cool.

The ride back if you were wise enough to apologize, and even then, God didn't harp at you the whole time.

The One who loves you doesn't need you to be perfect to ride with you. It doesn't need to be a fair-weather, top-down day for God.

Even now, Dear Friend, God is riding shotgun. The truth is, God's always been there, ready to take over the driving any time you're overcome or under the weather. Maybe you've already given God the wheel. Maybe you have yet to believe it is possible.

Either way, your car is in God's care and headed home. Home is more wonderful than you, I, or any of us can possibly conceive. Shotgun or behind the wheel, be loved, Beloved. Be loved.

30

WASHING AWAY THE MARKS
YOUR BURDEN LEFT BEHIND

The load has been heavy, Beloved. The loss of loved ones, left behind possessions, dashed hopes and dreams. The burden of undue expectations of yourself, the labor under the lash of "I should be here, I should be there, I should be doing this, I should be doing that." How many times did you carry the baggage of "I feel as if I am never doing enough. I am too much?"

When we can no longer take our self-lashing, we sometimes turn the lash on others. We have used a lack of forgiveness to keep us safe and ingratitude to keep us equal, all snuffing the light of our inner being, that place where we know and are known, that place that speaks for God.

All these expectations have been stuffed tightly inside the pack on your back labeled "inadequate." None of them were put there by the One who made you. Indeed, you were made to travel gently, nimbly, and creatively with a light step and a smiling heart. You were made to lend a hand without a thought and show up at parties poised to revel and rejoice.

Do you know what your Creator, the One who loves you, is inviting you to do right now? Drop the burden—let it slide off your shoulders. There's nothing left to accomplish except absorb the adventure. Human expectation is no more.

Step into the sluicing, warm goodness of God's love. It's like a soothing waterfall softly smoothing away the soreness, the redness, and the concave indents that the straps of such a burden leaves behind.

Feel the lovingness. "I made you and never once stopped loving you, Child."

Feel the healing. "I have loved you with an everlasting love. My love has always been the only thing necessary." (See Jeremiah 31:3.)

Feel the shift in your being as you stand straight and look at the One who never left, who holds out a hand and says, "The night is well spent, the morning comes. I will guide you home."

That One is with you, Beloved! Right now. Receive the caring and compassionate love of God. Receive the goodness, tenderness, loving-kindness, and understanding that leads to a long, assured forgiveness.

Rest, abide, and welcome the love of God. Lay down your burden and be loved, Beloved. Be loved.

31

IN THE CLOUDS,
A DIFFERENT STORY IS TOLD

Love is in the air. You have only to look up into the sky to see it. The sun shines continuously, playing with the density of the clouds as they pass in front of your gaze. The light dims at times as it dives into the thickness only to illumine the edges, shining bright, the silver lining that says the light hasn't left.

The light hasn't left. It can't. Not you, me, or anyone, Dear One, can change that. The light can only shine upon all.

God is light. In God, darkness and light are as one. The Light is shining along a vast spectrum in many ways and rays we cannot see. Even the universe surrounding us is its own substance, Dear One, a fabric of time and space from which light is never voided out. It holds billions of galaxies our weak eyes cannot see.

Dear Friend, God's light is your light now. It has always belonged to you, for you have never once been without it. It is here right now, loving you, calling you to come and trust it. Find rest now, even right now, and let yourself be cared for down to the innermost depths of your being. God is there, full of life. God's mercies and affection ceaselessly abound, some unseen, yet always more than you could ever use up. They are fresh every morning and freshest "some glad morning." (See Lamentations 3:22–23.)

The clouds don't tell even a tenth of the story, Beloved. They are parting now as you rise in grace. You can see it in the light on your face. So much behind you. So much more to come.

Love awaits like the sun behind the clouds.

It is here, shining the same glory from which you were conceived, Child of Love. Abide in God's light and be loved, Beloved. Be loved.

32

TEARS PRECIOUS ENOUGH
TO SAVE

God will meet you at the threshold, holding your tears in a bottle—a bottle God designed especially for you. The tears collected come not just from your eyes. God also collects the tears of your heart, Beloved.

The tears you couldn't cry when someone tore into you physically, verbally, emotionally, spiritually, or mentally, and you didn't wish to show weakness.

The tears you couldn't cry when circumstances demanded you act with dignity.

The tears you couldn't cry when times were hard, and you had to set your mind and hand to the task ahead of you for the good of those who relied on you.

The tears you couldn't cry when being strong meant hiding how you felt to free another.

The tears that came cascading down when waves of sadness came crashing over you, often when you were least prepared for the smash, causing the floodgates to open.

The tears you couldn't cry for only the reasons you know. God knows them too and has honored all that you went through by saving them. The One who loves you does this to assure you your trials had a constant witness. Each and every time you sorrowed after loss, each and every time you suffered pain, each and every time remembered by the One who made you.

"I know, dear Child," God says, swinging the door to home wide. "I know. And I understand. Welcome home. As precious as these tears are to me, no more shall come to you here."

The embrace of your Creator feels like love in all its wondrous forms but in a unified whole. The One that is love itself, the One who ushers you inside, keeps this promise: There are no tears in God's home. You are about to enter the house of the only One who can turn life's floods of tears into baths of resuscitation and showers of restoration.

Beloved, the time for tears is coming to a close. Here, you are free to love as you have always wanted to love—deeply, lavishly, and joyfully. This is the will of God. This is your true inheritance, Child of God.

Receive.

Let God take it from here. God will, Beloved, for God wills.

Be loved, Beloved. Be loved.

33

THE OFF-RAMP LEADS TO EDEN

The road has been broken, hills have been climbed, tumble-downs into rocky ravines have been survived. All have led to this place where you might think it all has ended. Indeed, Beloved, this is only the beginning.

If everything holds within its limitless possibilities, be assured that your transition is without measure. Made by the eternal God, you are bound for eternal love. It is the love that has always been with you and with me. Inside that eternity is love expressed in ways we cannot fathom.

We tend to compare it to our own. God's love is so much more.

But here you are still, broken down in a way, your body pulled over to the side of the road, it seems. You are not. You have been taken to the off-ramp, Friend, where at the bottom the garden awaits, the garden that is God's.

Eden.

Moreover, you don't need to drive the car from this moment forward. Sit in the passenger seat. Lean your head against the cool glass of the window. Gaze into the stars, each one a sun, each one a light of the One who made you, the One who loves you, the One who loves us all. That One is at the wheel now, Beloved.

Your eyes may close, drowsy, as the journey winds to a close. "Rest, sleep, abide in love, Dear Friend," God says. For all is well. Eden is just around the bend.

You are loved, Beloved. You are loved.

34

A SONG OF GOD'S FAITHFUL LOVE

LORD, your faithful love reaches to the sky.
Your faithfulness is as high as the clouds.
Your goodness is higher than the highest mountains.
Your fairness is deeper than the deepest ocean.
LORD, you protect people and animals.
Nothing is more precious than your loving kindness.
All people can find protection close to you.
They get strength from all the good things in your house.
You let them drink from your wonderful river.
The fountain of life flows from you.
Your light lets us see light.

—Psalm 36:5–9 (ERV)

BOOK 2:

WORDS OF HOPE TO READ ALOUD WITH THOSE IN CRITICAL CONDITION

"I know you by name.
I have loved you with an everlasting love."
—God

To all who are created by an infinitely loving, limitlessly able, and perfectly knowing God.

35

THE PEACEFUL FLOW

Receive the healing flow of God's love for you, Beloved. It's always gushing out of the heart of the One who made you. This love stream is so powerful that if you but realized it fully, you would place yourself beneath the unending flow every moment of every day.

This love doesn't crash upon you or smash you down. It settles like a stream of silken water that somehow restores and refreshes, even as it cushions and comforts you in its depths. The love of God cannot be plugged or pinched. It is given to you, me, all of us, never running out, always filling, fulfilling, and finding.

Feel the flow of it upon you now, especially now, Beloved. No matter how incapacitated, your body is giving its all in this extreme set of circumstances. The future is on your mind. Let it be one of life and recovery. The love of God, flowing freely, is your greatest accompaniment. Rest peacefully in the active, awing love of God. That love is the greatest healer in existence. That love is always there when you are ready for it.

This peace won't harm you or take you to a place where the "fight" is gone—indeed not. This peace, past your understanding but always in your favor, is your strength and shield. This peace, a precious and precocious gift, is the confidence that you have placed yourself in the healing hands of a tender and trustworthy God. This God is the One who loves you unconditionally.

Unconditionally!

God loves you, Beloved. It's true! God really loves you, me, and all that the Creator made.

Breathe in the love.

Let the love of the One who is always with you flow over you as it will. Feel it envelop you, and then let God do what God does best: refresh, restore, enliven, and make whole. Your "Yes" is all that is needed. God will take it from here. What a comfort, a companion, and a loving presence our Creator is for you, me, and all of us. In this healing flow of goodness and grace be loved, Beloved. Be loved.

36

A VISION OF LOVE

God sees us, Beloved, not just as a patient observer, a being that watches clinically like a researcher, or in fascination like a spectator. God is more than a watcher, an observer, a wonderer, or a ponderer. God's seeing of us is like a benevolent witness. When nobody else sees your struggles, sacrifices, and quiet acts of goodness, or the times you suffered in silence—God is there.

The One who made you will never abandon you, Dear Friend. You have never left God's sight. Indeed, you cannot leave God's sight. The One who loves you with endless love will never leave or forsake you (see Deuteronomy 31:8). How can one be fully, eternally loved without being fully, eternally known? God's seeing is God's knowing. God will come to your aid when you ask for it. When you're unable because you're weak and wounded, you only have to receive what is always offered.

Because God knows us, we don't have to hide anything about ourselves. We can be vulnerable and authentic. The One who sees and knows you wants a totally honest relationship. You are already held in God's gaze, the unflinching omniscience of the One who created you. All that is in the eyes of the Holy God is love.

Love has set its eyes on you, Friend! You are so worth loving to your Creator, as am I. This love heals, restores, and fashions your life into a thing of beauty. You can trust it. It is worthy of your confidence. This trust is good for all times, seasons, and circumstances. The reason you can trust God? God has seen it all. More than anybody else, even more than you, God knows what to do best to deliver you. God knows your next best step.

Imagine the most loving pair of eyes you can, Beloved. They behold you as a parent, a good parent, a strong parent, a helping parent who will guide you with greater ease when the struggle for control is laid aside.

Be seen, Dear Friend! Reach forth your hand and rest fully assured that God is not here to hurt or punish you but to heal you in perfect ways and timing. Rest. Rest patiently and calmly today. Luxuriate in the love of the One who sees you as you are. This love, fully flowing, knowing, and seeing, is the most complete and perfect love you can ever know—and it's yours.

Be loved, Beloved. Be loved.

37

ALL THE RIGHT MOVES

Ask God to help you, Friend, and God will. Perhaps you've asked God to do just that in the past, and it feels like God left you high and dry. It feels that way for many of us, chiefly because we want God to follow the blueprint we created for God to help us.

Imagine if we did that sort of thing to an EMT. "Please keep me breathing, but don't use oxygen to do it. Please staunch the bleeding, but no direct pressure or tourniquets. Please fix my leg, even though my arm is broken." Any EMT who listens to the patient's demands might as well go home.

When the One who loves you doesn't respond to you like you think you deserve or like you think you demand, it's for your good and not your hurt. What we think is best is often shortsighted and shorthanded. When God answers our prayers, God applies the tourniquet to the right place, often bandaging a wound we didn't know we had. Our bind as humans is failing to recognize the divine bandages and medicinal bindings. We are so prone to believe in the world's definitions of "success"—Wall Street money, Hollywood beauty, Disneyland relationships—that we feel deserted by God when help fails to arrive in our preferred timing and through the world's prescribed lenses.

When we ask God to help us and then trust God for the perfect diagnosis and treatment, with no expectation as to delivery or method, it's like letting an ambulance crew staffed with the best physicians, paramedics, nurses, EMTs, and drivers do what is best to give us emergency aid and therapy.

At this moment, it might be tempting to pray to God with a companion list of how-to and what-next questions. Let them go, Friend. Let God be God over you, in and through you. Relax and drop your defenses. Let God reign now, and rain down on you showers of power, blessing, and strength.

Let the struggle you've entered invite you to draw closer to the One who made you. God is ready to help and knows exactly what you need, when you need it, before you know it. While you're at it, let God love you to the fullest. The One who loves you unfailingly is the God who heals you, the greatest healing source there is or ever can be. God hears your prayers, tracks your tears, holds you, and enfolds you. Allow yourself to be upheld, uplifted, sustained, and delivered into wholeness.

Be loved, Beloved. Be loved.

38

THE LIGHT

Friend, wrap yourself today in the warmth of God's love for you. In a world where everything is transactional, God's non-transactional love may be hard to accept or apprehend. Just like Linus's blue blanket, we can grasp the real security blanket of God's love, because God is love. God is also light—even the darkness is as light to God. (See Psalm 139:12.)

Truly, God's love lights your existence and can shine in your heart even now, illuminating the love that is already there, shining from the image of God within. As long as God's light shines, yours will not go out.

Receive the love of the One who made you, me, and all of us. God's love is given, not as generic love but as handcrafted love that is custom fit for you, perfectly optimized for how you were created.

It is like stepping outside after a prolonged storm; the darkened skies have been pierced by God's love. Its laser focus goes straight to your heart, warming its walls with the light of forgiveness, freedom, promise, and strength.

But like any good giver of gifts, that's not all! The light of God is so much more than the singular focus that can set your heart on fire and on a sure path. The light of God is over all, colorful and sweeping, arcing like a rainbow over your entire existence. Even when the world feels dreary and lonely, the night seems long, and the path ahead is shrouded in mystery, the beauty of God's light is all around you. Is it an accident that after a storm, rainbows appear?

This bow of light in the sky isn't martial or meant to be strung with an arrow. For the bow of God, Beloved, rests above us, arching its beauty as a sign of God's promises. The rapture of colors in the sky, the radiance of resplendence, the dance of light in the atmosphere—these are expressions of the love of God for you. The myriad ways our eyes behold this glory are the myriad ways in which you are loved.

This grand and glorious love is never changing in essence. But it is displayed in countless hues of affection—sometimes passionate red, sometimes cuddling blue or joy-filled yellow, and every color of nature in between. God's love is yours in an eternal, delighting, enlivening, enlightening, leavening light.

Be loved, Beloved. Be loved.

39

THE DIAMOND

God's love is like a diamond. It is old, deep, and bright, a perfect gem nesting peacefully below the earth's surface. But just as diamonds are pushed closer to the surface by seismic and volcanic activity, God's love is ready to spring to the surface of our lives at the most trying times. Upset and upheaval make diamonds easier to find and easier to unearth.

Unlike a diamond, though, God's love can find you. Open your eyes to its brilliance, Friend. Look upon its luminous presence and realize the love diamond of the Divine is the hardest, hardiest substance in the universe. This is why we necklace, bangle, and bracelet this precious mineral on those we love.

A diamond maintains itself. It can't be broken down by acids and toxins that leech into our lives: cruelty, indifference, impatience, prejudice. Elemental forces like unforgiveness or tit-for-tat transactionalism are used to keep equilibrium, but at what cost? The price of our freedom, the loss of our joy.

God's love breaks through all of that by telling us several things:

You are loved no matter what. The unchanging, unconditional nature of God's love, impermeable to our human errors, doesn't crush under pressure and isn't scratched by the littlest offense. God's love for you, me, and everyone maintains itself. Beloved, God's love for you, was, is, and always shall be diamond rock-hard. God loves you as the child of the Creator that you are. It is a love on which you can bet and build your life.

God's love never fails.

God loves to love with and through us, much like when other elements are mixed in during the formation process of diamonds. Blue, canary, and brown diamonds take form, uniquely beautiful and singularly diverse. God will love you, Friend. Even now, as your body and mind are interlocked in procedures of radical restoration, the love that comes to you now will continue with you once this session is finished. There's no telling what beauty you, me, or any human can create when our intensive process in the formation of love is over.

Beauty is only part of it. God's love cannot be scratched or worn away. It is the perfect diamond, stunning in its luster and lastingness. Like the diamonds we wear, it is already perfectly faceted, shining love upon all in countless points of light.

Beloved, it is upholding you now. In all things God's love is contained, for God loves all God created—including you and me. That precious love is the setting as well as the stone. It is ageless, timeless, and priceless. God loves you, Friend. God loves me. You can't out-love the Creator.

Let the diamond's resiliency welcome you, its strength support you, and its adornment astound you. Let its deep, enduring care for you whisper its words of life, wisdom, and healing. Abide in and attend to the love being born in you.

Be loved, Beloved. Be loved.

40

THE SHIP

God is like a sailing ship upon the waves of life, taking us to harbor on days when we need the calm waters of who God is. In the ship of the One who sustains creation, we find a strong keel upon which all is connected, the beauty, the goodness, and the truth of what life can be. When we step aboard the vessel God provides, it is always good.

A ship can be home, too, a boat on which we brave and venture through the world God has created. We find the mast and sails that will catch the wind on this craft. And on this ship, we may adjust the mechanisms. Swing the rudder this way or that. Change the coordinates. Our will is something the One who loves us unqualifiedly does not thwart.

But there comes a time in life, Friend—yours, mine, and everyone's—where we might say, "Take the tiller, God, and place Your hand around it. My will is what You want, my wheelhouse what You desire for me." A good journey is assured when the sails grow taut with the breath of God's Spirit.

In the most stormy seas, God is the most skillful sailor of the craft in which the Creator placed you long ago at the inception of your being. The One who is with you envisioned the places you would go and the experiences you would have together. When God sails the boat at just the right pitch, the hum begins. When a ship is in perfect tandem with the wind, sails unfurled, that ship hydroplanes. You can hear the levitation by the sound of the hum, the music of God, and you are off together.

By placing God's hand at the tiller, you desire the rudder to be in harmony with God's loving Spirit, a Spirit that doesn't trick or tempt, a Spirit that resonates with what you are fully capable of right now. If we find ourselves in rough seas, who is better equipped to guide the boat flawlessly than the One who created everything? Love like God's—steady, assured, ancient, and experienced—is full of promise and will not put you upon the rocks. Oh, no! God leads you into places of peace by the still waters, along coves of protection, and into ports of provision. Your life is love's landing. Love landed in you, on you, and through you. Look around you, Friend, through the porthole of God's love.

The One who is with you is ship, wind, and sea. God, the All in All, is the most skillful sailor, able to cut through storms and carve a path through the most threatening waves that are crashing on you right now.

Feel God's love around you each moment. Abide in it as it takes you to the place the One who holds you has prepared for you, a place to heal and be well, where you know you are loved. Be led to harbor now as you heal.

Be loved, Beloved. Be loved.

41

THE DOOR

God's love is the door through which everything must go forth and come back home. When we forget God, we lose sight of the immediacy of the eternal access to the most beautiful, most good, and most true.

Through the door of God's love, you can enter into a place where you may receive love the way God gives it: unconditionally and eternally, without regard to whether or not it comes back or how. For love that keeps score like that isn't love. When love arrives through the door of God, you can let go of all you had hoped to accomplish alone and allow the One who made you to have complete access to all your hopes, dreams, and cares.

The door of God's love invites you to a place wherein you, me, and all God's children may enter at any time, bruised, broken, or proud. God's love never fails anyone.

"Leave your bags at the door, Beloved," God cries. "I will provide for all your needs now."

Leave the disappointments, the fears, the reliance upon others' opinions that are not true. God is true. Leave the losses you still cannot understand. Freely enter. Freely stay. Freely let the One who made you provide for all of your needs. Freely let God heal you, Dear Child.

Does this seem impossible to you?

Friend, even when you cannot leave all your baggage and enter the holy of holies in trust where we see only God, hear only God's voice, and walk firm-footed in God's way of beauty, truth, goodness, and love, God will come through the portal of time and space. God will sit with you in your disappointment, pride, and need for others to see you as you wish. God will take your hand and say, "I'll never leave you or forsake you, Child, for my love is from everlasting to everlasting." (See Psalm 103:17.)

God loves you on either side of the door because God is everywhere and knows exactly who you believe yourself to be, who you truly are, where you have found yourself, and why. God can do none else, for your Divine Parent knows all.

In times of great distress, when you cannot even see the door, it is always next to you, in front of you, behind you, and in all directions. You may say "Yes" to God no matter where you are, and God will help you step through the door. God will enable you, by God's unassailable love, to realize this good news: all that awaits within the surrender of laying down your life as you have known it is for your good—for God is good. God will help you see beauty in its fullness— for God is beautiful. The One who loves you will help you hear the sweet and perfect sound of God's voice that always speaks the truth so you can listen to the drumbeat of God's heartbeat: I love you.

Love is the door that says, "Come in and be loved, Beloved. Be loved."

42

THE LIGHTHOUSE

The love of the One who loves you unconditionally is like a lighthouse abiding on the rocky shore. Its light sweeps over the restless waves threatening our good passage. God's love beams over the storm and says, "I will light the way, so rest. Rest, Child, rest."

Like the rescuer that lives upon the rocky shore, God comes down from the lens room, pulls the rowboat into the roiling surf, and circles the oars as if they are nothing. The tempest means little to the Almighty. The One who made you holds out a loving hand, inviting you to your rescue.

May you heave a sigh of relief and pray, "Oh, blessed Keeper of my soul, I'm in Your care now."

Once again, God tells you, "Rest now. I Am come aboard your lot. I Am come to the storm. I Am lighthouse, boat, and sea. I Am your strong and steady passage to calmer straits. I calm the waters."

When life becomes too much, and control is wrested away by tossing waves too wild for your powers, only lift your wrist and take God's arm. You are now in the perfect position for your Creator's balm of divine love. That love is your home and mine, our lighthouse, today, tomorrow, and every day, we say "Yes" to being carried by God, rocked and cradled in omnipotence, leaning on the everlasting arms.

So light my path with Your love, O God, even as I trust in You. Take me to tranquil straits and secure bays. Your love provides me with all I need for safe passage. Part my waters, move my sea, still my storm.

Be filled, Dear Friend, with God's healing presence, and in that, within and without, you will be loved, Beloved. Be loved.

43

THE LONG-FORGOTTEN MEMORY

God comes into your life many times like a whirlwind, many times like a long-forgotten memory. We are told by the wise to leave the past behind, and it is assumed that left behind are the hard, painful things that happened to us. Perhaps we also need to leave behind the fallout of decisions we have made that we cannot go back and change.

That is excellent advice as you keep as much stress away from yourself as possible right now. It's true. Focusing on the past and continued rumination on how it could have been different will change only one thing: your ability to live your life right now. Be generous in your forgetfulness and gracious in your remembrances. Let go of memories that fatten on grievances, jealousies, rivalries, and injustices.

In this time of intense repair, God will come to you, Friend. God will come to you in long forgotten memories of kindness, goodness, and closeness. Allow the One who knows all things to show up right now as the people who have loved you in your lifetime. God always shows up in loving people, for where love is, God is.

Perhaps it was loving parents. Perhaps a neighbor you escaped to when you were a child who loved you and gave you good snacks. Did you have a special teacher who took time with you or a coworker who invited you to eat lunch with them? Let them come to you now, Friend. Ask God to bring to your mind all the people who made a difference in your life in whirlwind ways or small practicalities.

It's not just the brain where memory is located. Memory resides in the whole body. Let your entire being remember. God will come to you in long forgotten memories of senses and places God created to begin with and God created for you to enjoy. Did you have a corner of your house where you read books or played games? How about your bedroom? Did you love sneaking away or settling down at the public library? Perhaps you might find yourself in classrooms where teachers took care to decorate large bulletin boards with lavish colors and shapes. Were there walks, hikes, or ball games? Swims in the ocean, lake, river, or neighborhood pool, shouting as you jumped the waves, laughing as you careened off the diving board. Even sitting in the sand on your towel and watching others play in the sun. Ask God to take you to those happy places that still reside in the hallways of your mind. Remember your rememberings that brought you out of isolation and separation.

The past can be a beautiful place if we avail ourselves of its memories. Not just memories of the hardness of the struggle, but remembrances of the holiness of the simple gifts, the divine blessings of kind people and pregnant places ready to give birth to the goodness of God in you.

God will come to you in all ways, dear Child. God loves you in a rush of timeless love. Allow God to redeem your life even now with a love that has always been there for you in ways great and small, like long forgotten memories that still fill your heart with joy. Discernment in knowing what to forget and what to remember determines whether life is a drag or a delight. Sink into those good rememberings and rest in the peace and promise of the One who loves you with an everlasting love, yesterday, today, and forever.

Be loved, Beloved. Be loved.

44

BENDING DOWN TO LISTEN

God is not just in the heavenly heights, as many of us have been led to believe. God does not look down upon us from a distance, examining our every move and weighing it on the scales of divine perfection. Friend, the perfection of the One who made you, me, and all of us is so great, so unable to be modified, God bends down to us! Yes, God gets down and dirty with us. With a listening ear, a loving gaze, and the whisper of the Spirit, God comes to us in our troubles, messes, and daily turmoil and trauma.

The struggle you are in right now is a giant one, Child of God— no doubting that. But did you know you are not alone? Yes, there are people attending to you: doctors, nurses, assistants, and aids. But behind the scenes there is a backup team of attendants, and administrators that keep the facility operating, dedicated people cleaning the rooms and hallways, staff keeping supplies ordered and stocked, and cooks making meals down in the kitchen. Within all of them, God bends down and touches you.

Yet, there's still more to the God that comes to you, Dear Friend. The God who is everywhere cannot help but be with you. Isn't that good news? God is not defined by boundaries unlike you. God comes to you, bends down and listens, because God is already here. In God you live, move, and have your being, from that vast outer space in which your body lives, to the equally vast inner space in which your atoms spin and your cells reside and replicate. Listen to the hum of life and the song of love. God's unbounded love is within, without, and all around you now.

Tell God your sorrows, and your struggles. Lay all those things into the hands of the One who loves you unfathomably. God will heal your heart. God will make a way when good ways seem to have gone away. God listens and forgives all you have done to hurt others, and yourself. God already knows your secrets. Let your truth, all you have done fall upon God's forgiving ears. God wants the best for you. God's mercies are as deep as the deepest ocean and wider than all the seas put together. God knows, and God *still* loves.

Free yourself and others in this moment, Friend. Forgive and recognize where forgiveness is needed. Lay it all on the altar of God's love.. Even now, God's ear bends to you. Tell God everything, not because God needs you to but because the truth will set you free (see John 8:32). Even now, Dear One, your Divine Parent holds you in the everlasting arms, surrounding you with reminders of the great love that has always been. It is always being extended toward you, sustaining you, and giving you life. Forgive, be forgiven, let go, see God with you here, and in all ways be loved, Beloved. Be loved.

45

AWAKE, AWARE, AND ABIDING

It's hard to imagine someone who never sleeps. We have businesses that never sleep pharmacies, grocery stores, and all-night diners. A person needs to rest—just like you do now, dear Child of God.

God never sleeps. When we are joyful, God is awake. When we are sad, God is aware. When we are suffering or rallying all our resources just to take another breath, God abides with you.

God is awake right now, Dear One. God is fully aware of everything going on in your life at this moment. Awake and aware, God abides with you, me, and all that God made and loves. There is an abundance in God's abidance.

God sits with you now, like a tender parent in the night when their child burns with fever, wiping a little forehead with a damp cloth, smoothing their hair, lifting their head to give them water, and speaking softly as their feverish dreams overtake them. God is with you, around you, and in your deepest place. The One who made you abides. God never leaves any of us alone, Dear One. Not for a single second. God never leaves you alone.

You are accompanied right now. Even in your dire moments where the fragility of life is most manifest, you are with the One who loves you unconditionally. God watches over you like a loving parent, awake, aware, alert, and abiding. Allow for God's presence that is always with you to love you, soothe you by applying balms of comfort and healing.

God will make known the power of the One who knows you fully, dearly, and entirely. God's great desire is for you to thrive in wholeness of goodness, beauty, and truth. The power of Love is here for you to abide in and sink down in when your own strength seems gone.

God sees you always—aware of your situation, attentive to your needs, and abiding with you. Let the peace that comes from knowing you are held in God's everlasting arms fill you, Dear Friend. The abiding One holds you, wiping every fear and tear from your brow, tenderly whispering words of assurance when the dreams and the fears become too intense for the healing you require.

God will take care of you. Let God take care of you and be loved, Beloved. Be loved.

46

THE HOUSE ON THE HILL

There's a house on the hill, Beloved, and it bids you welcome. You made quite the climb to arrive at the peak on which it rests, overlooking the landscape before it. It's the landscape of your life, the landscape of who you have come to be, and who has journeyed with you. Rocks have been climbed, detours negotiated, cliff faces navigated. Dark nights spent in forested areas and raging waters crossed, you have climbed and climbed, most likely more than you would have liked to at times.

Whatever your journey has been like, whether one of plenty or scarcity, whether rich or poor in friendships or funds or time, you are invited to step across the threshold of this house on the hill. On the doorpost the word LOVE is carved in big letters. This is your house of healing and hope, Child of God. There's a house of healing and hope for every human God created. You don't get there by demand or force, but by two simple words to the One who loves you, "Help me."

With that open sesame—"Help me!"—the door swings wide. The night is pierced with light and warmth. Deep in your heart you enter this haven of rest. The One who has always been with you, welcoming you, is ready to give you everything you need, even needs you don't know you have. "Sit down, take off your shoes, and feel free to put your feet on the coffee table," God says. "Supper's almost ready."

God pours love for you like wine into a glass, Beloved of God.

God pulls a roasting pan of comfort from the oven, dear Child of God.

God sets a pot of healing on to simmer in the background, full of fruit and spices that fill you with heavenly repair.

God says, "Eat, Beloved. Fill yourself with My nectars and nutrients of healing grace. Drink in all that I have for you, to give you goodness, to give you life." God loves you, Beloved. God loves you, me, all of us, with a love we can't out-love.

Oh, the generosity of our good Creator!

This house has been built for you—right now, right here. Rest in love. Abide in love, the love that is from everlasting to everlasting, the love that will never let you go. Be loved, Beloved. Be loved.

47

A LONG COOL DRINK

When we are thirsty, we drink. The drink satisfies our mouths and throats. It gives us relief from the superficial effects of a lack of hydration, but a drink does so much more once it hits our stomachs.

After air, water is the next most important substance we need to survive. Our bodies are mostly made up of water. Not to drink is, finally, not to live. When we feel parched, we find the refrigerator or a spigot. We open our mouths and willfully swallow. A very good decision as we submit subconsciously to the design of our Creator. Hydration is built into every system we have, down into our very cells. Our body allows for liquid expulsion as well as daily intake of fresh water.

God's love is like that, Dear Friend. Your willingness to receive it opens the floodgates for love to go from the tiniest opening to the deepest belly of our being. Love seeps into all our systems: companions, confessions, emotions, motions, motivations, and perceptions. Imagine floating in love, splashing in love, diving in love, and dog-paddling in love.

God is always ready to love in, with, under, and through you. Even now, here, in these extreme portions of pain and seasons of suffering, you are not without divine care. God made you and loves you. God created you to experience the living water in all its forms of liquid, ice, and steam. Drink in the love that has been the life of the cosmos since before the dawn of time. This love is eternal, everywhere, and enough—no matter what, where, or who you are. This love is God. God is your one and only Source. In God's love you live, move, and have your being. You live in Love-land with streams of living water all available.

Of God. From God. In God. With God. Under God. Through God.

Drink in that love, dear Child. Let the eternal fountain flow. Let it hydrate your being as it courses through you in all things and all ways. The Living Water is caressing you deeply, floating you now, and turning your salty dead seas into sweet rivers of life.

Be loved, Beloved. Be loved.

48

CHILDREN AND THEIR TOYS

One young child in innocence might love to show you her toys. Another might drag you over to the refrigerator to see his drawings, usually of houses and heroes, often of sunshine and rainbows, sometimes of scary siren heads or long, friendly horses. They might show you a dance, sing you a song, or even throw open the bottom drawer of the refrigerator to reveal their sippy drinks. Children naturally want to draw you into their world to see all that they love, revere, think is wonderful, and can do.

God, in divine innocence, is much the same. We can come as the child of God to receive the gift of God's love. Even here in this place you have found yourself—God delights in you. The One who made you looks upon you as a favored creation, part of all that was declared "good" upon the making of the universe. When God speaks of you, the Creator speaks of who God knows you to be. Lay aside all your mistakes and all the times you forgot God and you hurt yourself and others. When all of that is stripped away, all that remains is you: who you are in your very essence and who God made you to be.

Your essence is never what you have done or what you have left undone. Your essence is you, the pure surface upon which the Light reflects its intended glory. The light of love—the love of the Light of the World—shines on you. You are never excluded from that light of love, whatever state or stage you are in. How can you be excluded when the One who is everywhere made you and loves you with an unfading and unfailing love?

God is with you now, Friend, even during this time of anguish and confusion. God is looking upon you now as a child looks upon the things they love. God's love will lift you up and hold you to the heart of the One who loves you softly and tenderly. God is holding you forth, even to yourself, and saying, "See, Dear One? See who I love so utterly? Can't you see My artistry? See who I think is sublimely beautiful? I created you, the only 'you' in existence. Your being brings Me such pleasure."

Receive that love—let it enfold you, defend you, delight in you, sustain you, and heal you. It abides with you now, right here, in this place, even in this period of your life.

Be loved, Beloved. Be loved.

49

THE APPEARING OF LIGHT
AFTER DARKNESS

The light of love shines upon you now, Beloved.

You know what it is like when a strong light suddenly appears in the darkness. How often have we been warned in the bedroom that a light is about to be turned on? So we cover our eyes with the blanket. Slowly we adjust, taking a minute or two before completely removing the veil. When we don't cover our eyes, when the light in its full strength shines in suddenness, we squint and shirk, temporarily blinded.

We acclimate slowly to sudden changes, light being only one of them. Sudden shifts in temperature we describe as "getting hit by a blast of cold" or "a wave of heat crashing over us." God's love can be like that.

The radiance of God's love, in its total generosity, grace, and goodness, is hard to take. People who give generously to us without a thought leave us awestruck. Those who help out with the heaviest items on moving days are titans. Even blessing bombshells, like winning the lottery or unforeseen fortune, leave people spinning.

Another kind of light, the light of dawn and dusk, sneaks up on us. Like that, God can be gentle too. Receive God's loving light on you this day. Absorb its dawning rays of sweet healing as you sit under the majesty, might, and power of the One who cares for you. Rest in the Divine Presence. Receive this everlasting love in a slow and steady stream like the light of a new day's dawning.

Watch the daybreak yet again, Beloved. Sit in the darkness and watch the sky as it lightens, that intense blue tapping the horizon lovingly on the shoulder, bidding it to waken. This is your day, Child of God. This is your time, even while your body is undergoing great tribulation, to receive God's restoration. God loves you so much—always has and always will!

Let the light settle on you, Dear Friend, and I will let it settle on me. May we actualize ourselves wholly in the fullness of this light as we accept more and more of it. Just like the light of dawn that leads to day.

This love of God upholds, comforts, heals, and blesses. In light of that be loved, Beloved. Be loved.

50

THE FINEST ARTIST

You are a divine masterwork, Beloved.

Portraits were once the most popular way of capturing someone's image. The subject would sit for hours as their likeness was gathered two-dimensionally on canvas with paint or pastels, graphite or charcoal. The medium didn't matter, really, because when the artist turned the canvas around for the subject, what was presented was not really what the subject looked like. It was how the artist saw them outside-in, not knowing them inside-out.

The best portraits are of people in intimate contact with the artist. We see flesh with folds and dimples, eyes with the glaze of passion or the spark of rage, hair mussed, and clothing in natural creases.

Ever wonder what people think when their portraiture pops up for the first time? Are they disappointed? Are they happy? Do they examine the image over and over looking for clues about themselves or the artist?

Here's something worth looking at—you. You are the subject of the finest Artist in the universe, the Artist who designed the whole universe and the "youniverse" of you. Let that shake your view of yourself in a wonderful way. It's true for me too, for all of us. The One who created us has created a three-dimensional, moving, talking, and living sculpture that is more beautiful in the divine sight than any Degas dancer or Michelangelo's *David*.

God looks at the "youniverse" of you and says, "It is good, beautiful, and true." Every cell, every organ, every bone, and muscle. All the art you cannot see and all the art you can. "It is good, beautiful, and true." Your hair and skin. Your hands and eyes. The way you smile, the way you shake your head, the way you sing or laugh. Even your feet. "It is good, beautiful, and true."

God sees you with so much love, Dear Friend. God looks at you clothed in the light of the Creator's love that has never changed, not once, in every single moment of your life. God's love for you illumines you as the beautiful image you are, the image in which you were made, and the image of the One who loves all.

You are handcrafted, wanted, and cherished by God in the fullness of your being and beauty—now, all day long, tomorrow, and into forevermore. Receive this beautiful love, Child of God, and know that God doesn't love you in spite of who you are or what you have done. The Artist who created you sees you with eyes that love you from tip to toe, that know your end from your beginning—eyes of grace and mercy. Eyes that tell you, me, and all of us that we are beautiful in the sight of our almighty Artist.

Be loved, Beloved. Be loved.

51

FOR ONE MINUTE

Lean back and rest for a moment, Friend.

Many of us heard these words as children—"If you would please stop talking for one minute and let me speak"—by someone who knew better, or thought they knew better, about our situation and problem. It's better to hear that, for sure, than to be ignored. One of the worst treatments a parent can give a child—or that anyone can give to another human being—is the silent treatment, or as we like to put it, turning a cold shoulder.

It is no accident that the ultimate punishment in prison is solitary confinement.

God is the kindest parent anyone could have. God's kindness is like the wind. You cannot see the wind directly, only its effects on what it comes to and caresses. You cannot see God directly as you do people, animals, and objects. But God is with us, always breathing into us, always shining love upon us, always gazing with affection, always ready to hear and help, and always sending out wordless signals to trust and obey.

Today is a day of physical struggle for you. Medical staff will enter and leave the room, charting the things they have done to help you turn your injury or illness around. Their treatments might include surgery and other forms of unpleasantness. Be assured, God is with you, speaking peace and comfort over you in words you might not be able to hear but, like the wind, you'll be able to feel.

You might say, "But I don't feel God. No matter how much I pray and pray, God is silent." Dear Child of God, quiet your heart and listen to the voice of God that speaks for you, not just at you, that sings over you, not just to you. In the hush of stillness, hear the hum of holiness and healing in the myriad ways God breathes the divine breath in, over, and through you.

Ask God to help you, Friend, and stop speaking long enough to hear the loving response. This communication isn't just call and response, dialing 911, asking a question, getting an answer, and waiting until the next problem arises to pick up the phone. Although, rest assured, God is always at the end of the other line.

Beloved, this communication is being still enough to know God is always listening to the cries of your heart and your life, waiting for you to ask in honesty and show even just a smidgen of willingness to receive the perfect help.

There is no cold shoulder. Only warm baths in kindness and the tenderness of family, friends, and strangers. All of creation sings, the stars tell of the Ancient of Days who is fresh every morning and holds no surprises but love, caring, comfort, and the power to do exceedingly abundantly more than you can ever imagine (see Ephesians 3:20). This One invites you to let go and rest as divine healing takes hold. Leave it in God's hands, who turns not away but will boldly face with you anything that life on earth brings your way—even this. God's eyes are never off you. Even in this darkness, God sees.

Embrace the quiet of God and incline your ear to listen in closely. God loves us all so much, Friend. You are loved with an everlasting love. Receive it as God longs to give it, with no instructions of your own given to the One who made you. Trust that God knows all things, has your back, and only has your best on the horizon, cold shoulder never turned.

Be loved, Beloved. Be loved.

52

WORTH MORE THAN YOU KNOW

It's hard to put in words how worthy of love you are to God.

One of the hardest experiences of being human is suddenly finding we were unworthy of another's love. Almost every breakup plants seeds of doubt as to our own person. What was it about us that was so objectionable? What was it about who we were that couldn't be folded into another person's heart and loved into something beautiful?

Sometimes, if another person is involved, we plummet into the comparison game, either puffing ourselves up by denigrating them or blaming ourselves by assigning shortcomings in every corner of our own being. In trying to make sense of what happened, we mistake incompatibility for unworthiness and metabolize rejection into abjection.

Oh, Dear Friend of God, the One who made you and loves you never looks upon you like that. God designed you specifically to love and be loved not only by others who can walk with you in magnificent and beautiful ways, but to be loved divinely. God made you to love you, to love you utterly and to the uttermost of the Divine's imagination and glory. What others fail to see about you, God knows. Your worth is found in the unassailable truth that God's handwork is never patchwork or piecework, guesswork or outwork, but masterwork! When God sees you, God sees you as the child you still are, the offspring of the Divine, made intentionally and uniquely to live in relationship with the One who made you.

Break the chains of comparison to others. Cut the cables that compel you to caw and claw your way into God's acceptance and presence.

You are worthy to be loved.

You are worthy to be cared for.

You are worthy to be healed.

You are worthy, inherently worthy, not because of anything you have done or even could do. Your worth doesn't depend on any others, the world around you, or even your own opinion of yourself.

You are worthy of God's love and care because God made you to receive it. You are merely fulfilling the divine delight of communing with your Maker, no matter what. Forget what you have done or didn't do. Receive God's love today, Friend. It is your birthright, my birthright, and the birthright of us all.

Accept your acceptance as God's beloved child. Bask in God's creating, sustaining, abiding, restoring, maintaining, providing, relating grace and glory. You need no affirmation of your worth by another human. Let God's amazing love heal you in your true worth. Let love lift you now. Let love wrap you in a divine embrace that, in truth, has always been there. In the arms of the One who deems you lovable, be loved, Beloved. Be loved.

53

JUST STAND UP

God upholds you right now, Beloved.

Living in this world, we easily feel we are floundering. Waves batter and buffet us, whether from social unrest, political upheaval, or economic barriers to the bountiful resources of the planet.

Our personal lives have experienced much the same. Other humans enter and exit, sometimes seamlessly, many times tumultuously, leaving lasting effects for years to come. Perhaps we live in a perpetual state of difficult personalities and relentless problems. No amount of convincing ourselves otherwise seems to help us come to a peaceful daily existence.

Now here you are, your body in peril.

Imagine a person floundering in such waves, calling out to the waves themselves, begging them to stop, counting on their cessation for peace. Maybe you have called out to others to come and save you, like a distressed swimmer crying out to a lifeguard.

Dear Friend, we can get so distracted by the waves that we fail to realize there is a foundation beneath us, in reach of our feet.

"Stand up!" the lifeguard cries. "Just stand up! You think you're in over your head, but you're not!"

There is an everlasting, firm foundation beneath your striving to survive, Child of God. There is a place where you can plant your feet, where your head and shoulders are above the waves. We are in the sea of life, Beloved, you, me, and all of us. You know better than anyone that it would be silly to say we are not met with challenges and detours. But God is planted firmly beneath you in waist-deep water.

"Stand up!"

The One who loves you is like the sea bottom, perfectly positioned to support you when you're too weak to support yourself.

"Stand up!"

The One who delivers you can stop your floundering from the ground up, despite the waves that assail you from society, others, and even your body.

Right now, a decision you can make is whether or not to stand firm on the good ground of the good Creator. The Lifeguard has spoken. "Stand up! Just stand up!" Rest upon the terra firma of God's providence and protection for you. Even when your knees give out, trust God to lift you up and keep you standing.

Child of God, you have never been without this firm foundation. You have only been buffeted by the waves, driven by the doubts, and cast about by the fearful expectations from a limited imagination of what it means to trust in the One who made you, the One who loves you, and the One who never lets you go.

Stand firm in God's promise and power to rule the waves, calm the seas, and bear you up at this time in your life. You can trust the One who cares for you because you stand upon unshakable and inescapable love. This is a steadfast love that heals, restores, and shines its regenerating rays like the light of the sun.

Be loved, Beloved. Be loved.

54

THE MASTER ROAD BUILDER

A road paved with love is your birthright, Beloved.

The master road builder knows exactly where the road begins and where the road will end. Imagine laying down the first mile completely unaware of what the next mile will need. Road builders scout out the course ahead of time, designing for the curves of the land, for immovable mountains, and for rivers and ravines. It would be unthinkable and very poor engineering to do otherwise.

Here in this life, we try as best we can to see the road up ahead. But we are not privy to what is actually going to happen in the future. No matter how many advertisements for investment funds and wrinkle creams tell us otherwise, life happens amid making plans. We do not know the future. In many ways, isn't that a relief? All that crystal-balling gets exhausting.

The reality is, Child of God, the One who made you will also lay your road. The One who loves you will make the road of life accessible to all that love can bring to you. The One who never leaves you will also accompany you down every road no matter how rocky and steep. You have only to embrace the reality that you are locked in the mystery of the unseen that lies up ahead. You have only to trust that this deep mystery in which you now find yourself is fully known by the Creator, even though you don't know what tomorrow or even the next hour might bring.

Beloved Child of God, trust in the One who abides with you, even now, step-by-step. Place yourself fully in divine care and rest now. Heal—be mended in mind, body, and spirit, and be reminded of a God who knows all things, loves all creation, and whose pathway is life and life abundant. God walks in the light and the dark, Dear One. The mystery isn't so much darkness and fear but rather knowing who sees the past, present, and future—yours, mine, and all of ours. God is able to make a way from rocky paths and a good road from blocked streets and dead ends. Trust in the One who is the way, the truth, and the life (see John 14:6). The path forward is found there—not your own goodness, your own strength, your own intelligence, or your own resources.

This Builder of roads is fully equipped to carry you down the divine highway to life and love in the fullness of the Divine Presence. On this road you will constantly and consistently be loved, Beloved. Be loved.

55

FEEDING BENEATH THE SURFACE

Beloved, let us picture ourselves before a morning pond. The sun glistens in silver coins and glittering diamonds as the breeze glides over the surface of the water. The water shimmies and shifts as a duck pops its green head from beneath the surface to catch the warmth of the sun above. Watch as the duck swims then dives again. And look! Where we thought the water barren of birds, more heads appear. These waterfowl, who visit the depths to feed, surface once again. They paddle about in the place you see them. But when they dive, they are no less there than they were before.

God's love is like that, diving to places you may not be able to see but are there nevertheless. When we allow the One who created us to love us completely, that love will go to the uttermost depths of our trials, to the heart of our broken relationships, and into the bottommost places of our lives. The One who loves us brings up that which will feed us and heal us in ways we might not see at first, changing our hearts, renewing our minds, and feeding our souls.

Dear Friend of God, you have only to stand still and wait each day as the love of God surfaces before your eyes. God loves you so much, the depths are no matter. God created the depths, heights, and all there is; and God created you to live in it all. You were created to delight in creation, to create with it, and to share that passion and joy with those around you.

Receive the gifts God will bring to you from beneath the surfaces of life. God doesn't drag you down or around as you struggle to breathe. This isn't God. God doesn't take away or destroy anything good and beautiful from your life. This isn't God. God is goodness, beauty, and life itself.

See the pond of your life, Beloved. Watch as God surfaces repeatedly. Watch as your Creator and Sustainer dives in the deep and finds food for you, brings up healing, for the darkness is as light to God (see Psalm 139:12). Even now, let God be God. Let God surface joyfully before you and know that when you cannot perceive the workings of the One who loves you unconditionally, it is because that One is diving deep on your behalf.

Be loved, Beloved. Be loved.

56

WHILE YOU LIE SLEEPING

You are loved twenty-four hours a day, Dear Friend.

God's love is like a ship at sea in the night. Picture yourself on a cruise ship. No matter if you've never been on one of these huge "party on the waves." What you've seen on television is enough. On the lido deck, twenty-four-hour buffets, bandstands, slides into pools, and all the accompanying deck chairs await you. On other decks, more restaurants are ready to serve you, including a large dining room where most guests gather for dinner. Lounges sprout up in various places for people to listen to more music, watch sports, or play games. Gambling casinos serve the riskier vacationers. There are theaters featuring musicals and comedians. Lots of music, color, light, and life. Staff bustle about saying, "My pleasure," and a cruise director tries mightily to make sure you have the time of your life.

Beneath the decks where guests eat and play, the cabins line up. Some have views of the sparkling sea. Others peek out at the inside of a corridor, smaller wombs where lights-out means darkness, and the quiet is dense when sleep closes your eyes.

While most guests sleep, the crew that sails the ship comes to life. This is the time when the grand boat travels to its next port. In the still of night, the boat itself becomes true to the task it was built for—to sail the seas. Nothing else matters without this. The engines thrum, their vibrations calming as they coddle each person in their bed. The seas rock the boat gently, making it a cradle for all who abide within and above its steel hull. All is calm and all is right when the good captain and crew take you to your next destination.

There are days at sea, too, when all activity revolves around the forward momentum of the ship. People settle into a day where the horizon sweeps farther and higher, and there's nothing to do but enjoy the journey.

You are on the ship of God's love right now, Beloved, the engines humming, moving you through the night. Rest in the ease of knowing that you have nothing to do but abide where you are, resting confident that God is taking you to a good port, a beautiful place, where wholeness can be found in the simple fact that you, Dear One, are a child of God.

God doesn't throw you out to sea in times of storm. You don't have to paddle for your life. God is paddling for you. Just allow the fullness of God's love to support you through this time, to sail you along the currents of this sea, and to know exactly how best to get you to port. In perfect ways. In perfect timing. Always loving you unconditionally.

God never needs you to be perfect to heal you, help you, or paddle for you. Or what would be the point? God only needs you to say "Yes," to stay in the boat, not to jump ship. Allow the One who made you to fire up the engines, control the wheel, and move forward on your behalf. This is what will bring you peace, even here. Do you hear the hum of God's love?

Be loved, Beloved. Be loved.

57

THE OLDEST, MOST HUMBLE, PROFESSION

God is your Shepherd, dear child of the Creator.

A shepherd in real life isn't like the romantic notion we behold in December when we view a nativity scene. Shepherding is a job for outliers, for those who don't mind not having a bath every day, those who don't mind sleeping outside or caring for dirty animals in places they are neither seen nor heard by other people. Most shepherds don't get a lot of respect by cattle ranchers and other animal caretakers either. In ancient times, two words often went together: smelly shepherds.

Like a shepherd working for the welfare of animals in unseen places, God will care for you. Without needing to preserve the reputation of divine glory in the opinions of others, God will go into the wilderness of sickness, injury, heartache, loss, sorrow, and grief. God will look after the welfare of the entire flock while seeing to your need, Beloved One. The One who made you, me, and all of us, will care for us perfectly.

God isn't worried about how others perceive what can and will be done on your behalf. God will climb the highest mountain to rescue you and ford the deepest river to find you. God will carry you back to the flock, left in good pasture with running water, to skillfully set your bones, tend to your wounds, feed you from the divine hand, and give you rest.

Beloved, right now, believe it or not, is the perfect time to be cared for by your Divine Shepherd, the One who loves you, however far you roam or rebel. God will care for you now. Lamb, ram, or ewe, it doesn't matter to the Ancient of Days. We are all lambs of God.

Bow to God's good care and allow divine love to heal you. Say "Yes" to the voice of the Shepherd who created all, knows all, and loves all, including you and me. The best thing you can do right now is bed down and rest in this tender care. Let a compassion so great it's hard to comprehend hold you in its arms.

It is there, dear lamb, it is there for you. In this fond, faithful, and wise care—care that finds you when you're lost, comforts you when you grieve, mends you when you're broken, and loves you in all times and all ways—in this tenderhearted care of the Good Shepherd, be loved, Beloved. Be loved.

58

THE SHADE BY DAY

When the sun is at its peak and the day grows hot, the rays of our star settle upon our skin and set our eyes looking for the nearest shade tree. We seek shelter beneath its branches. Somehow the same light that burns our skin when we expose ourselves too long is the same light that nourishes the tree and grows the leaves that render our relief from its burning beams.

Beloved, God's love feels like that in many ways. It is always in our presence, able to avail itself in ways that seem contradictory to us. But love is, in fact, complimentary to itself. The beauty of God's love for you is that, while you are free to flit around or abide in its various aspects, there is a more sure way of availing yourself of its goodness, beauty, healing, and loving care.

Let it come to you.

Beloved, the One who made you is perfectly capable of loving you exactly as you need right now—yes, even in this place where you might feel at the mercy of those around you. God's love for you is something you can trust if you allow yourself. Let it nourish you like it does the trees. Let it shade you when it's time to be still, protected, and receive. God knows best what you need.

It's hard to imagine that, isn't it? Most of us take back over too soon after giving way to God's way. We decide not to wait until word is given, opportunities present themselves, or signs are displayed—like the parting of the sea, the straightening of our path, or the spotting of a lighthouse or shore in sight.

The One who loves you unconditionally is always aware, always moving creation toward goodness, beauty, and the truth that you are loved, I am loved, we all are loved. Each sheltering leaf can grow in the light of God's love for you—leaves of healing, grace, forgiveness, purpose, wholeness, and connection. Each leaf has only to be received because God's love is never something we earn any more than we earn shade from a tree.

Isn't that the best news?

As you rest, as you receive the ministrations of medical staff, housekeeping, and administrative personnel, know each one is like a leaf, sprouting from the shade tree of God's protective love with you now. Accept it fully, all of it, Dear Friend of God. It is always there for you like a mighty oak spreading her leafy branches over your head.

Be loved, Beloved. Be loved.

59

GOD WILL DO
THE HEAVY LIFTING

Rest now, Friend.

We are conditioned to think that every good thing must be earned and every good gift returned with one in kind. We tend to think God feels that way too. But the mercy, compassion, grace, and love of God for us, beloved children of the Divine, are so great, deep, wide, freely given, perfectly nutrified, and circulated that the thought of repayment is impossible.

God doesn't expect the impossible. God does the impossible.

God doesn't demand we behave ourselves, think rightly, or do great feats of righteousness to earn God's love. If there is any truth about God that is hard to accept, this is surely one. For if this is true, that God loves everyone, all that God created, we must accept something hard to accept. We must leave room for God to love all that blow across this earth leaving a path of destruction and sorrow in their wake. God doesn't mind us misunderstanding such grace, for how can we comprehend a God who doesn't need our love to love us?

Friend, the good news about God's unconditional love is that the One who made you sees everything about you and offers something just as amazing as this incomprehensible grace: the invitation to cast your burdens on the Creator's shoulders and say, "Take my life and make of it something better, something more akin to what You designed me in love to experience and express."

Let go of your burden, Dear One. There's nothing more to be done right now. Nothing you need to accomplish today. Let go and let God, the One who is with you always, do the heavy lifting for you. This is "Godlove."

This is the love that judges not, steps in, heals, and changes everything. We only must decide to receive it, to be changed by it, to reset our life to reflect not who we think we are but who God knows us to be—designed to love and be loved. This is ease, this is flow, and this, Dear One, is surrendering the weight that has grown too heavy to bear.

Ask God to shoulder your burden right now. Hand it over to the One who loves you—all the baggage, bottles, and fifty-pound sacks. Hand over your healing, hurt, sorrow, regrets, anguish, pain, and feel the weight lift. And you know what? God will carry you too! Right now. The divine arms are everlasting arms, fully able to bear you up. In this divine embrace, leaning on the everlasting arms, be loved, Beloved. Be loved.

60

LIKE A FOUNTAIN

God's love is like a fountain, drops of water descending like diamonds, glittering in the vast, indiscriminate light of the sun. Each drop charts a course of its own. Propelled by the pump inside the fountain, scattered in various directions by the day's breeze, they collect together with countless other drops into the basin. Each drop gathers together in a place called God's eternal love.

Beloved, you are invited to thrust your hands beneath these drops of love found in the minutes of your life, every moment under the sun, every breath beneath the moonlight, put there in grace for such a time as this. God's love has been with you through it all. Each drop, each moment of your life, has brought you here to this moment.

Some drops have fallen like the pelting of rain on a blustery night. Other drops descended like the benevolent settling of the dew at dawn, alighting on the fertile field of your existence. The ever-flowing fountain has endowed you with life, with a will of your own, with unending opportunities to love and be loved. No drop of water has gone to waste, for all can be used of God, even now, Child of God. Especially now.

Receive that which falls onto you, each drop collecting into a stream of healing light, of loving song. The fountain of life is:

always the same, and always changing;

always still, and always in motion;

always old, and always new;

always gentle, and always powerful.

A fountain has a single source with no beginning and no ending. A fountain breathes out and in, moves up and down, at the same time.

Bathe and bask in the Fountain of Life itself, that flows from the very heart of the One who made you. This waterfall of love will wrap you in arms that bear, protect, and squeeze you close in grand affection.

Feel the healing refreshment within you and allow it to spread to all the dry and frozen places that have forgotten how loved you are! This love is the basis of all joy that you have ever felt, all the beauty you have ever seen, and all the fulfillment and peace you have ever known. The basin of this fountain collects this one unforgettable fact: God has always loved you and God will always love you. Receive each drop of love. Let it pool in the basin of your heart and let it heal. From the inside out, let divine love be as it will: perfect, whole, and wanting only your good, my good, and the good of all. For God's love is so great, no one is left dry or thirsty.

Be loved, Beloved. Be loved.

61

THE TRUE IMAGE IN THE MIRROR

Beloved, it's not what you look like that matters to God. God made every child of creation unique. The mirror tells but little of the tale. Your worth comes from a much deeper place than your physical appearance. You are worthy because despite what might seem otherwise, the child of God, like the child of a human, bears the image of its Parent. The design for you, Dear One, is this: to receive an outpouring of love so bountiful, beautiful, glorious, and full of grace and truth that it could only begin in the mind of the One who dreamed you up in the first place.

In this mirror of God's gracious love, your true image is reflected. All of it, Beloved, is the image of your Creator. There is nothing you can do to be more beautiful. God sees you through the eyes of a love so comprehensive and compassionate it only recognizes that which is eternal. Grace pries away all that stands between you and the realization of who you truly are.

There is a username for that person in the mirror: Child_of_God. There is a password for life with God: love. You, dear Child_of_God, were made to love and to be loved by God. All that God made is good, beautiful, and true. Look upon yourself as God looks upon you—worthy of life, love, restoration, good relationship, and union with your Creator. Receive that love for you now, Child of God, creation of the Light. You reflect the image of the One who was, who is, and who is to come. When you receive that unconditional love, it will do the work for you. It will melt and mold you into the creation you truly are.

In this time of healing and repair, know you are worth everything to God. God does not hold your good over your head as something to be deserved, only something to be received. See God in the mirror.

Open your heart to love. Your true-life inheritance is before you. The divine image looks upon you from within, always ready for you to say, "Yes."

Be loved, Beloved. Be loved.

62

THE SUMMER FIELD

Come into a field in summer, Beloved.

The sky overhead glows from its blue heights as if more than the sun lights its great expanse. Lay yourself down, rest amid the carpet of soft grass covered by the velvet petals of a million golden flowers. Everything soaks up the slanted rays of the late afternoon, all still refreshed from the morning rain, now evaporated into clear air moving over your face, legs, and arms.

In this field, life burgeons like a living fountain, giving birth to more life. Little bees visit flower after flower gathering pollen, replenishing the lushness of the ground and the branches of the nearby trees with their industry, season after season. A field is a place of fertility, new life, cycles great and small, surprise, and growth. Child of God, rest here in this place where hope is birthed in the healing you now desire. The One who is with you now lavishes healing liniments on you in all ways, touching your body, heart, mind, and spirit all the way down into every layer that you are.

God made and knows each place where wounds abide.

Let the sun of God's love warm you now. Breathe God's never-ending grace inside your lungs, clean, clear, and perfect for you in every moment. Listen to the hum of life—life abundant, sweet, and beautiful. Feel the purpose of living each day in such wonder as the summer field can bring. The One who loves you utterly has created a world for you to inhabit and enjoy. Picture yourself in it now, Beloved, breathing deeply, eating your favorite food, drinking, laughing, loving, and looking forward to tomorrow. For in that tomorrow, as well as today, you are unconditionally loved by your Creator, as am I, as are we all.

Remember to live today, Beloved. Remember to love right now, deep inside your heart, Dear One. Experience the abiding presence of God and be loved, Beloved. Be loved.

63

A TREE HOUSE WAY UP HIGH

In many ways, Friend, you are in a world unto yourself at this time. While everything bustles around you and people care for you, please know that in this place you have found yourself—deep inside where your thoughts are yours alone—you are not alone.

God is with you. God is holding you.

It is as if you are in a tree high above the world, in a canopy of oaks, the leaves glistening, dappled in the sunlit drops of freshly fallen rain. Breathe in the fresh scent of new-fallen rain. Inhale the aromatic woods of the walls, floor, and ceiling.

Child of God, you are with the One who lavishes love on you and pursues you with that extravagant love. You are with your Maker who knows all that you have been through, everything you've done, and loves you with the fullness of divine grace, mercy, and compassion. God made you to live in joy, peace, and wonder. God made you to receive all-consuming love, all that you can hold in any given moment.

Here in this little place you share now with God and God alone, rest, Beloved. Rest in the surety that God cares for and about you deeply, so deeply.

Let the world spin and hum. Let all the people in it go about their busyness. But you are here now, in the haven within built by your Creator, made at your very beginning. You share this space inside your heart with the One who loves you more than you can possibly imagine.

In this still place in a spinning world, in this room high above the din, in the green canopy of God's good, healing, and affectionate company, be loved, Beloved. Be loved.

64

LEAD KINDLY LIGHT

The journey you are on right now is not an easy one, Beloved. It's a journey far beyond your control or understanding. You may be feeling as if the uncertainty of the outcome is more than you know how to handle.

But I tell you this, Friend, there is a candle burning in the darkness. Its flame is bright and steady, its clarity providing more warmth than it seemingly should. In this light is the healing power of the One who made you, me, and all things. In this light is the knowing of the One who loves you, the One who created you to live in joy, sleep in peace, and walk each day in love. This holy light has been with you since you began your journey. This true light, this light of the One who knows you better than you can even know yourself, will guide you and guard you, even now.

All you need to do, dear Child of God, is feast your eyes upon this light of love. Allow its grace simply to fall upon you, to seep into the marrow of your bones, to recognize itself deep within your heart. The light within you is the light that shines in the darkness. It is the image of God, which has never left you, Beloved. God's light has never not fallen upon you in mercy, truth, and compassion.

Feel that light within, without, a flame burning through the darkness, burning like a star, leading you through the mystery of this time in which you have found yourself. As Byzantine poet Symeon once said, God's light "shines on us without evening, without change, without alteration, without form. It speaks, works, lives, gives life, and changes into light those whom it illuminates."

Change into light:

See the Light.

Receive the Light.
Walk the Light.
Send the Light.

Be the light and be loved, Beloved. Be loved.

65

YOU CARRY ALL THE LOVE YOU NEED WITH YOU RIGHT NOW

Imagine you always have with you a backpack filled with all you could ever need. Imagine it weighs nothing. For though it is with you, it is held by the One who created you. Imagine that its contents are perfectly ordered so that what you need, when you need it, is right there at the top, ready for you to pluck out for its intended purpose. This pack is never a burden. It is there to bring you peace, purpose, and pleasure.

This backpack is like God's love for you: always present, always promotive, and always prepared to bring you exactly what you need in God's perfect timing. Inside that backpack is healing grace, the grace of God that says, "Yes, My Child, I want you to live free from pain, free from suffering, abounding in My great love for you. I created you to live in this kind of freedom no matter what others may say to the contrary."

Reach inside, Beloved One, and know that what you pick is perfectly placed. Trust what is there for you now. It is the gift you are meant to receive. Let it come as it will. "God's clock keeps perfect time," as the old saying goes.

What you are always meant to pull out of that backpack is God's love. The encircling, encompassing, empowering, empathizing, emboldening, emancipating, and embracing love God has always meant for you to receive. There's nothing you can do to earn it. It is with you, around you, under you, and in you always. All you need to do is say yes. Yes, I receive Your wondrous and amazing love. Yes, I accept the Love that made me. Yes, I acknowledge that Love made me intentionally, not as a mistake, not as a fluke, but with a high and holy design from which I can never be parted.

Beloved, your backpack is perfect for the journey you have undertaken, in easy times and hard times. Enjoy it, unpack it like the treasure chest it is, and share its bounty and blessings with others. This abiding love is so great you can spread it around, dispensing its peace, knowing there will always be more since its source and supply is unending.

This love is with you now, on your side, restoring, reclaiming, and reconciling you to what has always been. Receive it, Dear One. Receive the care and goodness of your God and be loved, Beloved. Be loved.

66

FACE TO FACE

Gaze upon the face of your beloved Maker, Child of God. It is always turned toward you. You see God's face in those who nurture, in the service of compassionate people who give and give without measure, without expectation of return. See God's face radiating with joy at your presence, for you were hallowed to wallow in the presence of the Presence.

The One who made you will never—can never—turn away from you, Child of God. God is omnipresent, seeing all that is—claiming all creation and calling it good. God created you to look upon you, to delight in you, to sing over you the never-ending song of union with your own "belovedness" in God's sight.

God's affection for you shows in the face of the Divine. See the eyes of the One who loves you endlessly sparkle in the light reflected upon all you see. See the beauty of God's shining countenance halo your loving caretakers and know that God sees you the same way. God sees the innocent child, the beautiful son or daughter that you are, in the completeness of who you were made to be. God sees you for who you truly are and what you fully can be in that which can never be destroyed, disfigured, or defaced. For it is the part of you that has never left your Creator, a part, perhaps, long forgotten.

Gaze into the face of the One who set the stars in the sky and charted the foundations of the earth, created your frame and all the intricate workings within. Within those eyes be loved, Beloved. Be loved.

67

"YOU ARE MY FRIENDS"

There is a Friend that sticks closer than a brother or sister, Dear One (see Proverbs 18:24). That Friend just so happens to be the One who made you, the One who loves all of you, and the One who calls you "Friend."

We fall in love. We make friends and build friendships. God's love is so strong it "friends" us into the very life of the divine. God's love is inescapable, for it is all around you, in every nook and cranny, every place to stand, and every wide-open space. It is the all-mighty, all-weather, all-knowing, all-encompassing, all-consuming love of God for you, me, and all of us.

What a friendship!

Lay in it like a bed of soft blankets and a customized mattress readied for you by your loving Friend after a long, hard journey. The Friend who says, "I put on your favorite sheets."

Stand beneath it like a shower of refreshing rain, soaking into every opening, both those made to be there and those opened up by the lashes of life. "Take as long as you need. There's plenty of water."

Enjoy it like a surprise party you've stumbled into, planned just for you because your Friend knows exactly what you were created to savor. "I made your favorite cake."

Look at it like a welcome sign that bids you stay in this place prepared just for you since before time began. "I know what you truly love, and it is here. Welcome home."

This Friend tenderly makes and cares for all. But this Friend is most seen and known by those who understand God's great compassion and care for them. Child of God, this Friend is right now with you, me, and all. Open your eyes. See the love inside you and around you. Trust the abiding love you have been inhaling all your life. Know this love as ever present, ever emerging, and ever eternal.

In this great love, this immense love of God for you, rest in patience and acquiesce in your ability to say, "Your will be done, my All in All." Believe it shall be done. Let go and let in the Creator's healing love. Open your eyes to its presence. God will take it from there—joyfully. God will take care of you—abundantly. God will carry you to a very blessed completion—perfectly. When that happens is up to you, Dear Friend. May it begin right now. In this beautiful friendship be loved, Beloved. Be loved.

68

GOD YOUR CHAMPION

The strong forgive and move on. The weak avenge, stew, and keep score. This is more true when the subject is you, and the forgiving is of yourself more than the forgiving of others.

Perhaps you've been told of a jealous God whose glory and honor need protection. Maybe you were given altar calls of lore about a retributive God who measures your every thought and action and, when weighed against divine perfection, springs into action against you.

Quite the contrary. Wipe that blackboard clean. The world measures you, but God treasures you. Some expect God to be as narrow, small, and judgmental as they are.

God knows you, Child of God. You are created in perfect love, in divine intention. You are made for relationship with the Creator and the creation itself. If the word *jealousy* can be used, it is that God is jealous for you. God knows that focusing on our shortcomings and our sometimes-downright inability to "do the right thing" does not lead to a closer walk with the All in All. Rather, it forces our frailty and pain to take center stage in our lives.

God wants you all to "Godself" and here's why, Dear One. Your guilt cannot change anything...but your victory in God can. Your unloving actions and the focus on them does not stem the flow of God's love for you, nor can it turn the tide for you...but knowing of your position in the everlasting arms will.

Do you see that even your desire to change yourself, to clean up yourself by yourself, is an errand akin to delivering a set of orders that only details the problem? We can go back over and chafe at everything we have ever done, every ill-chosen word, every illicit thought, and every ill-tempered lie that set us up on the throne of our own hearts and minds as our own god. But there's nothing in doing so that actually helps. It's like fighting a battle with toothpicks.

We can bear shame, we can carry the unforgiveness of ourselves and others like an armor so thick and heavy we cannot move. God's plan for you, Dear One, for me, and for all of us, uses none of that. Do you know how much God desires your freedom? Freedom from the past, freedom from fear, freedom from anguish, and freedom from shame and guilt?

Many years ago, knights, clad in full suits of armor, would be hoisted onto their horses by a kind of crane. Sitting on that high horse gave them the idea they were impermeable to the arrows of others while meting out judgment with their own swords and lances. God will gently take you down from your high horse now, Beloved. God will lift that heavy armor for you so you might walk about in freedom and joy.

Forgive. Give all you have ever done to God, who will judge it as ineffectual against God's own desire to clutch you in the divine embrace. Be forever held in divine affection close to the very heart of God. Forgiveness is the gateway to fullness of life. Gratitude is the roadway on which fullness of life is experienced and expressed.

Forgive. Don't try to live a forgiven life or struggle to live out your forgiveness. Your life already is a forgiven life. Surrender your flimsy sword that will never find its mark, and let the One who loves you turn your sword into a scalpel and heal you wholly. Sound the "God-into-your-hands-I-commit-myself" cry of peace. Brave the "It is finished" ceasefire. Sing the "I'm home!" shout-out of serenity. Raise the white flag of surrender to God's championing goodness knowing fully you are loved, and then be loved, Beloved. Be loved.

69

A SONG OF GOD'S FAITHFUL LOVE

Don't worry—I am with you.
Don't be afraid—I am your God.
I will make you strong and help you.
I will support you with my right hand that brings victory.

—Isaiah 41:10 (ERV)

BOOK 3:

WORDS OF LIFE TO READ ALOUD WITH THOSE IN DEEP DESPAIR

"I am always with you."
—God

To all still hoisting the chalice of hope in the midst of your suffering.

And to those who found the chalice of hope too heavy to lift.

In memory of Chris Nielsen
May 7, 1988

70

THE GUEST OF HONOR

Welcome, Friend. You are received joyfully and with full acceptance into a home like no other.

I invite you to picture the most beautiful dining room you can. Fine woods, like ebony and mahogany, have been carved and assembled into tables and chairs. A colorful carpet overlays shining flooring. Lights glitter and sparkle amid paintings from the hands of the finest artists the world has ever seen, from east to west.

Have a seat, Beloved.

Around the table sit a variety of human beings. Perhaps your physician is there and a teacher you admired. There are celebrities who dazzle us and scientists who have made life-changing discoveries. People born to great wealth and ease, dressed to perfection; athletes who push the boundaries of the human body; and explorers of untamed wildernesses. All share the same kind of salad you do, same soup, same entrée, and dessert.

The Host stands up, raises a glass, points to you, and says, "Everyone, welcome our honored guest!"

What is this? Why am I here? A lot of us would ask these questions in the presence of such human illustriousness.

It's easy to compare ourselves to others and produce reasons why we are better or worse. This can lead us to false conclusions about our Creator. The truth looks more like this:

You have been invited to the table of God, Dear One. But instead of the accomplishments, physical prowess, beauty, and social standing that we humans tend to value, we gather as one. One body of humanity, one family of God. And yes—you, me, and each one of us—are the guests of honor. You see, God has no favorites; we are all supremely honored. How could we not be? We were made by the Host, the same Host who, after creating all that was made, declared, "It is good."

Humanity is God's honored guest.

At this table, Friend, we don't really sit with the wealthy, witty, or wonderful. That scientist holds the pain of childhood abuse. That actress cared for her terminally ill mother for years. That teacher showed up early every day to help students who were struggling. That wealthy socialite bore up under crippling depression and answered a suicide hotline to keep herself alive. There are others who seem to have given their lives to addictive substances, hazardous relationships, nursed grievances, delusions of impossible expectations, and compulsive behaviors, and yet...they are honored too. You are honored. I am honored.

Do you understand, Friend? When God looks upon you, God honors you just as much as anybody who has ever walked this world. The Creator's grace and favor emanates to all. Those who accept their place as God's honored guest eat of the bounty of God's table and allow hallowed nourishment to fuel their lives and everyone else's too. At this table, the extravagant truth that "we all do well when we all do well" is evident.

Beloved, the truth is, you are already at this table. Mostly, we have turned our chairs outward and have forgotten where we rightfully sit. Turn to the table, pick up your fork, and feast on the love of God, the milk and honey of heaven.

Be the honored guest that you are.

Let this festive feast be what it is for you, come to you as it will. You don't have to go into the kitchen and tell the cook what to make you. That would defeat the purpose. Trust in the nourishing, revitalizing, and mending menu of God as it manifests before you, around you, and in you. True, you don't have to eat anything; but at least try everything God sets before you. You may just be pleasantly surprised. As you sit at the table of divine bounty, goodness, and grace, be loved, Beloved. Be loved.

71

LIFE FORCE AND FORCE OF LIFE

One of the biggest mistakes we can make in life is to confuse our ways with God's ways. One of the easiest ways to do so is to imagine a Creator of limited resources or to conjecture a miserly Creator who only metes out blessings upon those who "deserve" them. If you doubt how hard we try to "deserve" God's favor and abundance, just check out any religion. But Friend, we cannot purify or magnify ourselves to earn God's love and power. That love and power is always flowing in great magnitude and multitude regardless.

Still we try. It feels as if we are self-sustaining creatures, doesn't it? It's not as if we plug a cord into a wall where life energy flows into us. We walk around, make decisions, choose our homes, fuel our bodies with food and water, and clothe ourselves in garments that attempt to tell others who we are inside. Our decisions become who we think we are. I only eat organic food. I only wear clothing made by the best designers. My tiny house or big house is better than yours.

Beloved, life is about so much more than food and drink, where we lie down and sleep, and what we are clothed in. When used as identifiers or means of holiness, we soon find ourselves living in severe limitation, even when all these things are the best money can buy.

Looking to the right and to the left, sizing up what others have or don't have, gives us false beliefs about where we stand before God. God blesses that man because he wears Armani suits and doesn't bless me because of my Goodwill clothes. That woman is on the forefront of God's grace because she successfully runs a business. Look at where she vacations! That car!

Stop. Breathe. Remember, Dear One. Remember that you originally came to this world inside a place where every need was provided from your mother. The temperature was perfect. Sustenance came in directly from the umbilical cord. Injury was very hard to come by.

But then, you were born. All that security went away, you might say, in that moment of birth.

But does it? The truth is, you are sustained by so much more than air, food, water, and protection. You are sustained by the very life force of the Creator, secured without measure and without merit. The life God extends, the force that invigorates your body and enlivens your very existence, is never-ending. Your soul is plugged into a plenitude of love and life. How much of that flow you channel and conduct is indicative of who you think you are, not who God is.

Open your heart, Friend. Try God and see. Receive a love so great it will never let you go no matter what. Your very existence depends upon that love, whether you realize it or not.

So realize that love; ask that it be made plain. When you pray to receive divine sustenance and direction, God will answer your prayer. You will come to see that this is nothing new and that God has been empowering you all along. You are not alone in needing grace to see it. I do too, and so do we all.

Open our eyes, O God, to see the loving stream of life You pour out upon us each day. May we receive it and let it strengthen us. Please relieve us of our misconceptions that You do not care, that You withhold Your goodness, and that You hide Your truth.

Let that change us, bringing us from darkness to light, and into a joyful heart, sound mind, healthy body, and loving spirit.

Amen.

In the beautiful Force of Life that is our God, be loved, Beloved. Be loved.

72

THE CORNERSTONE CRADLE

Y ou were once cradled in the arms of the Creator's imagination. That's how special you are. Your Maker breathed into your face and proclaimed, "You get life." What a gift. With the exhalation of the divine "You get life" comes the inhalation of the divine "I got you." This cradle and existence, coupled with relationship, is also your cornerstone.

Our beingness began with the laying of this cornerstone. Your cornerstone is still set firmly in place. God is always ready to lead you back to it, out of the chaos, out of the realms of fate, chance, time, and mortality.

"See here, Child?" God says. "This is who you are. This is who you were made to be. This is who, with My help, you absolutely can become." You answer, "But I can be such a dunderhead." God answers back, "But you're my dunderhead." You say, "I am one who finds the dunce's cap a good fit." God replies, "I made you and love you, even when you're performing below your best, being a dunce and dunderhead."

We can look upon the shambling house that we've built and others have torn down, or we can return to the original stone, laid with the original blueprint of beauty, truth, and goodness. Do you know where that blueprint begins, Friend? What is on its first page? One thing only: receive the love of the One who made you. That's all the very first drawing is. That's all the very first step can ever be. You are worthy to receive the love of your Maker, for that is your number one reason for being! The good news is...you were made for love.

As part of your acceptance of your reason for being, God will show you what stones to remove from what you've built and in what order, and which stone to lay next, and the next. Stone after stone.

All true to the cornerstone, each day will reveal itself in divine timing through love and lovingkindness, through faith and faithfulness, through hope and hopefulness. Opportunities to say "Yes" to the Divine Builder will come. Trust in God's three-storied architecture for every human life. First, a love you can receive in any given moment, challenging or easy. Second, faith in God's wanting only good for you. Third, hope in a future that can overcome any past.

Return to who you are, who you truly are. You are loved and formed and set in place by the One who made all things including you, me, and all of us. That which is built upon your cornerstone will stand strong, no matter the weather or the quakes. For your cornerstone is set into the solid rock that is your God. Build upon that rock and be loved, Beloved. Be loved.

73

MORE LIGHT THAN MEETS THE EYE

In God there is no darkness at all. In God we live and move and have our being (see Acts 17:28). Therefore, no matter how dark the night seems, how long and exhausting, we are always in the light. No matter who tells you the light is gone, you are still in the light. Friend, we close our eyes to the light all the time and proclaim it is dark. No time is it easier to do this than when the hard-core trials of life crash down on us: death, loneliness, loss of job, home, finances, and relationship. Loss tells us it is dark. But darkness, Friend, is a myth.

What is dark to us is not dark to the Creator. Our place of despair is God's place of repair. Our jumbled mess is God's opportunity to make straight. Our darkness is not dark to God.

Our darkness can be an invitation to the One who loves you unconditionally to shine new light upon your path. Not just your path, but on you, Dear One. God's light of mercy, justice, humility, and kindness might feel like an invitation to stand still, to remain just where you are. It is, Friend, it is. Partly.

Be still and know God is God (see Psalm 46:10). Stand still and see the salvation of the Lord. Watch the light shine from without and within. Behold the deliverance of your Creator, by your Creator, from your Creator, as truth is revealed in the light of God's truth. And the ultimate truth is this…you were made by God, you are loved by God, and there's nothing you can do to change either of those realities no matter how hard you try.

It takes patience to allow God's perfect light to manifest itself in your life. We want to jump in and do it our way, don't we? But here you are, here I am, and here God is. God the Stronghold will guard and guide your first step. We never have to do it alone in the dark, of our own strength. We can't. If we could, we wouldn't need God's help.

Friend, God loves you so much, God will meet you in your darkness. Your Source, Strength, and Song is poised to shed more light, more spark, and more sparkle than your wildest dreams, those dreams you've abandoned, tamed by fear and time.

Let the Light shine. The darkness is not dark to God. God will you help you see. In divine light, be loved, Beloved. Be loved.

74

SURRENDERING TO PEACE

In wartime, waving the white flag means surrender. When there's nothing left to do but die with the enemy surrounding you, giving up means staying alive.

Not so with God, Friend. Not so with God.

God is never an aggressor moving in to seize your free will. God will never take over the heaven-ordained territory that is your life here on earth. Perhaps you've grown up with the idea of a vengeful, narcissistic god who's only out for god. Our God's glory however, can never be less than it is. In all our restlessness and recklessness, we as humans certainly don't hold one bit of power to dim its beauty, brightness, beaconing, and beckoning.

What is the ultimate truth of God's glory? It shines upon all, and its ultimate end is joy within itself—and with you within it, in full realization. You shining in all your created and creative potential, hand in hand with the Source of Joy, the Source of Love, the Source of All. The All in All.

In your joy is found your peace, your shalom, which is the full and abiding peace of God.

Peace in itself, Dear One, is an outcome of surrendering yourself to God's glory, God's love, and God's intent for your life. Self-surrender is the path to self-fulfillment. Lose yourself in service to find yourself in freedom. Scientists have trouble explaining altruism: they can understand hostility and violence but have trouble understanding why we are kind to one another. That can only be understood in the light of humans being made in the image of the Divine. To surrender to the One who made us is to find the calling God placed on your life. God calls you, summoning you to move and to mission. God calls you, not because you deserve it, or even because you're good. God calls you because it pleases God to call you and bring you alongside the Creator to love, enjoy, and work with creation.

Hold up the white flag that doesn't say, "I give up," rather "I have surrendered to the Highest Power, my Lord and my God." To surrender to God is to embrace your relationships according to the mission of love and peace, not hatred and violence.

Friend, raise your pristine flag as the signal of your reliance on God for each day. Trust that the power of the Divine Presence is prepared and eager to put you back together again. Forget all that Humpty Dumpty nursery trumpery. Your caring is your curing. Your tending to others puts yourself back together again. Your service is your filling of those cracks. The King of Kings and Lord of Lords can do what "all the king's horses and all the kings men" couldn't do: put Humpty back together again. Piece by piece. Step by step. Hour by hour. Day by day.

Loving act by loving act.

Reach out, Friend. You have others in your life who are feeling despair, are sick and lonely. When they take your offered hand, you bring them into a new land where hope is alive because you are alive, they are alive, and God is alive. God is alive, Beloved. God is willing to lift you up to a place of surrendering to divine peace, love, guidance, and joy. You will be surrounded by those who you helped, those who saw God in you.

In this joy that is coming, be loved, Beloved. Be loved.

75

THE SUN SHINES AS IT DOES

Although this isn't a researched, documented statement, one might assume no human has ever changed the sun. But no mind. We change the trajectory of the light that flows from the sun all the time. We direct it with glass and mirrors. We magnify it into something able to carve a path of heat and fire. We diffuse it with shades or block it out altogether with curtains. But what we can never do is change the sun at its source. We can only receive it as we decide what to do with it, as is our God-given right.

Oh, Friend, Child of the Light, the Light is always shining. The Source of Light never grows dark, gives out, gives up, or rescinds its flow. The eternal and life-giving light of God is the love of God. It shines upon us all. God loves everyone, Beloved. God loves you, me, and all of us. Unlike the light of the sun, which is one day destined to die, God's love is unending, unrelenting, and fearless of rejection by you or me.

You were created to grow and flourish in the light. You were created to receive the light-filled love of God. Step into the light, Beloved. Receive it as it comes. There's no need to shade it, block it out, or place your own lens between it and yourself. That only guarantees a burn or a burnout. This light is what you are made for.

This light will:

Enlighten you.

Enliven you.

Enlarge you.

Enlist you.

And will never let you go.

All it takes is, "Yes."

You see, Friend, when you let the Light be as it is, you learn to shine as you are too. No more shining in accordance with faulty expectations, arbitrary weights and measures, or fleeting and fussing preferential strictures. You are free to stand as you are, as the Light has revealed you to be...a child of the Creator, created in God who said of all things created, "Wow!"

Stand in the Light. Placing your feet in the circle of trust, look up, let it flow upon your face, and light up your steps. Knowing it will never end, be loved, Beloved. Be loved.

76

THE KEY OF HONESTY (PART 1)

Beloved, your honesty with God is key to unlocking the door to a more truthful and fruitful reality. In times of despair, we can lock our gaze on our trauma and loss, bear grievance with what is behind or around us, and feel defenseless. The way society (and religion) honors perfection, we have been told we must meet certain expectations to warrant God's participation in our lives.

Friend, if we could do that, we wouldn't need God's help at all. But there can come a day when you, me, and every human can turn to face the Creator with every piece of baggage we own—everything we've done, every word we've said, every thought—and drop them in front of us.

"Here, God. Here's the truth as I see it. It's the only truth I have, and I might as well be honest about it. I'm disappointed. I'm despairing. I'm self-centered, not just in my self-pride but in my self-loathing. I can't stand living. Other people drive me down to the grave. If You were more on the job, I wouldn't feel this way, would I? Would I? I don't even know that.

"I'm in the dark most of the time. I ask and don't receive. I seek and I do not find. I knock and the door isn't opened. If this is the way life is, count me out. I'm too scared to do anything about that other than die a slow death here inside myself. It's dark, it's cold, and where are You? What am I missing? Please tell me what I am missing. By the way, my body hurts too. My partner is horrible. The government is way too out of control. Don't even get me started on religion either, God. Why do Your people act the way they do if You make such a difference?"

Maybe we feel once we get started, that's all it will ever be. Sorrow, pain, grievance, and more of the same until we die.

Beloved, God already knows how you feel. God is with you in all of it. God has been with you since the inception of your soul and the conception of your body. People say, "God can handle your anger," and it's true. But God can also take your honesty, even if your honest side is brutal or grounded in misperception, miscommunication, and mistaken identity. God already knows how you feel and loves you with no shadow of turning, those feelings notwithstanding.

Do you see? You can, you know. Knowing you are fully loved and completely known by your Creator is fully possible.

In that most true of all divine-human truths, be loved, Beloved. Be loved.

77

THE KEY OF HONESTY (PART 2)

The use of the word *frankly* signals an underlying "unfrankness," as if the person were holding something back. Same with the word *honestly*. But when you are honestly honest with the Creator about how you truly feel, you open the gateways of communication both with yourself and with the Divine. It may hurt to be so honest and real. But that honesty key opens the door to the place where the One who made you abides, the place where you can admit it's beyond you now, and the crippling sadness can start healing. Tell God the truth, and God will have truth to tell.

With greater and greater honesty and vulnerability with God, God can get real with you, Friend. The reality of God is: God loves you and will help you when you cry out. God will not only save you from all the lies you have told yourself and others but from all the lies others have forced upon you too. It's like unlocking all the potential truth and reality life can hold for you. It can start with the knowledge of one thing—God loves you. You are the site of grace in spite of who you believe yourself to be. In any given moment.

When you turn to God and tell the honest truth, you start down the path of trust. God is good, Friend. The Creator delivers lovingkindness and tender mercies to all who call upon the One who loves without limit. And in this honesty, you will not only come to speak of your sorrows but see your blessings too. It's important to be honest about what we have, what we are given, and how we are cared for to live a more accurate reality.

David, the poet-king of long ago Israel, wrote with psychological honesty about despair, depression, loneliness, and trust. He trusted God listened and loved. Like David, turn the key. Speak from your heart, your mind, and your life to the One who carries you, me, and all of us to a place of peace, life, and joy abundant. Knock, seek, ask with the key of honesty, and be loved, Beloved. Be loved.

78

THE TREASURY WITHIN

The Tower of London sits on the banks of the River Thames. It boasts the distinction of never having been overtaken by an enemy force. People have been executed in its courtyard, even murdered within its walls. Also within the Tower of London, kept safe there for many years, are the Crown Jewels. One man tried to steal them but never made it out of the fortress.

The Crown Jewels aren't simply precious for their monetary value but also for their relational symbolism. These precious items belong to the King of England. That alone is enough to value their safekeeping. They have never been insured because they are priceless.

Beloved, you belong to the Ruler of all. You are every bit as priceless to the Creator as the Crown Jewels of the Royal Collection are to the monarchy of England. In fact, to God you are more valuable than the sovereign's orb set with rubies, emeralds, and sapphires. The Earth can give up more diamonds, rubies, and emeralds, but you are one-of-a-kind precious. You are God's treasure, the wealth of heaven, one of the crowns of creation itself.

If you are as a precious gem to God, it goes without saying how precious you are—period. God didn't create you to wallow in wretchedness, disgrace, confusion, fear, helplessness, and hopelessness. Dear One, God created you to be free to shine. God created you to receive divine light and love, to glow with the flow of the Creator's steadfast lovingkindness.

The days of beating yourself up can end. Let them go. The days of consigning yourself to the dirt—let them be a thing of the past. God made you to be unearthed, glittering in sublime revelations of the Divine's love for you. Look upon yourself and see what God sees. You are an intricately carved treasure meant to glorify creation and your

Creator. You are created to be in intimate relationship with the One who made all treasured things.

You are worthy to God not because of your good behavior but because God intensely loves you. Is life worth the living? Yes, Friend, yes! Not only is your life worth living, but you are of priceless worth. You may think you're more trouble than you're worth, but your worth is inherent, never earned, never begged, bargained, or bartered for, never measured, only realized. You are a child of the King, offspring of the King of Kings and Lord of Lords. You bear in your being a royal inheritance.

Like all good gifts, the true and authentic you is something you must receive. You are like a fine necklace from a monarch, or a deed of land from the governor. Your gifts already are. You already are. You have merely to stand before the Giver of all gifts, hold out your hands to the great I Am, and say, "I am here."

Does it take trust that God can and will make you shine bright like a diamond in the sky? Absolutely. After all the years of neglect, after all the covering up of shame, blame, and lies, after the arid and airless concealments, the process of shining up the stone can take some time.

The first step is knowing you can shine. The second step is saying yes to shining. The third step is trusting God to do the cleaning and the buffing because God knows how to polish you in the most gentle and effective way possible.

Be the treasure you are. Take hold of your own creation, who you were made to be, and present it to the Creator to be fashioned into glory upon glory. You can do this, Friend.

Be loved, Beloved. Be loved.

79

THE SWING

It seems as if walking with two feet on the earth is the only way we can achieve some sort of stability. Beloved, maybe you feel as if the ground has been taken out from underneath you, like a table-cloth removed by a magician from beneath objects on a table. Only the trick was a failure, everything was upended, and where do you go from here?

Friend, there are more ways to be supported than this. God's love will support you from above even if your eyes are on the ground.

Look up above the muck and mire that is threatening to consume you. Perhaps it's circumstantial—loss of your job, your home, your most intimate relationship, or the death of a loved one. Perhaps it goes deeper than that as you seek not just to live with trauma but to be alive, and to experience joy in the journey.

Look up and live! Look up and behold God's love for you, anchoring you like the bolts of a swing attached to the beam overhead. God's love is suspending you. Pull up your feet; allow God to hold you. Trust that the swing you are in will remain firm. But trust nonetheless. When you put your feet down in the swing, the movement stops. But God's powerful love will uphold you and keep you moving in ways that, when you give the Creator the greater say-so, will lead you from the slog beneath your feet.

Just hold on. Just hold on. Grip the ropes from you to God. Hold the chain, for it is a lifeline, not a fetter. Stay here today and let God hold you and push you gently. There will come a day when you'll be swinging in wide arcs shouting, "Whee!" That is how you were made. Can you feel the wild yet controlled movement? Can you see the sweeping vista in front of you as you swing into the blue of the sky?

The air you will feel upon your face, your front, your back, when you are firmly held from the fingers of God, will refresh you. If you pray for eyes to see the blessings of each day as God desires to bring them, each day will compound itself in love. Bask in the sun, bathe in the rain, delight in the sustaining power of food that comes your way. Receive with gladness the love of those who God has sent or will send. Rest in it, lift your feet in it, move in it, be supported by it, and know it is always there for you.

Be loved, Beloved. Be loved.

80

HARMONY

My Friend, picture yourself in a music hall. A singer steps from the darkness onto the stage. As a singular light falls upon their costume, into the silent spotlight a note is gifted to the world. The clear note of the soloist pierces the air straight to your ear. The impact feels magnificent, and your breath catches. The pure tone, the true note, swells your heart.

If that isn't enough, a second arrow of sound strikes a note as another light falls upon another singer. The note harmonizes with its predecessor. And when a third person joins in the song, a certain replete joy makes its way inside of you. Yes, yes. Your heart expands yet further, almost aching. There is a harvest home to harmony. The beauty of harmony comes from simultaneous participation of unique parts in a manifested whole, note for note, beat for beat, word for word.

God made you to sing in harmony with all God is, all God created, and all God loves.

Your note, while beautiful on its own, was meant to be sung in chorus, expressed in community, and explored inside the canopy of creation that embraces us all. So too, my note. In short, I need you to make my note even more echoing and beautiful, and you need me.

What do we need sung the most? The first note of creation, the pure preexisting refrain of our Infinite One. This is a song voiced by whales in the deepest oceans and by birds in the highest heavens. This melodic line is sounded in a concurrent loop of infinite diffusion and infinite inclusion, all harmonious with our Maker's big chord.

We need you. Do you know that? Really know that? And truly how much? Humanity needs your note to be complete. What is more,

Beloved, there are people who absolutely know that God made you the way you are, to sing creation's song in your unique way.

Someone gave you this book, or is reading it to you now, adding their note to yours. Sing, Beloved, as only you can. Those who wish to sing in harmony with you and the anthem of creation will show up. I promise you, God is already singing with you and singing over you. In the Creator's song, of which you are a loved, beautiful, and indispensable note, be loved, Beloved. Be loved.

81

THE KEY TO EVERY LOCK (PART 1)

Ever wonder if locksmiths get addicted to that rush of relief at their presence? What must it be like to show up and always receive such a high appreciation rating? Is there anybody you'd rather see when you're locked out of your house, your car, or a box you found in the attic? Twenty-four seven service? Even better.

You've been looking for the key to your own well-being for a long time, haven't you, Friend?

Someone once said that the book of Psalms is a heap of keys that can open every door in a great city but that it's hard to determine which key opens which lock. Ever since the first human, serpents and sheep (some in wolves' clothing), people and programs, wise ones and self-help sages dangle rings and rings of keys, encouraging us to try them. Sometimes these keys fly in our faces, hitting us painfully, telling us things like, "You're too fat. You're not motivated enough, educated enough, or beautiful enough. You're not disciplined enough. You're not spiritual enough. Where's your pride? Don't you want to be better than you are, even equal to God?"

Perhaps you've dieted, educated yourself, climbed up the ladder, gathered all kinds of material possessions, eaten the best foods, consorted with the coolest people, or talked your head off with friends. Still here you are, with a handful of keys you've yet to try. Yoga, perhaps. Meditation. Politics. Art. Music. Finding a group that will welcome you. Even quick fame is achievable with the springboard of social media influencing. So yes, more followers, please. Fame seems as good a key as any.

We both know how many rich and famous, beautiful and bountiful people have led lives of inner despair. Because, Friend, when we get down that far into ourselves—and we do, Beloved, we do—there is only one love that will go down that far with us. Your Creator is the wellspring of this love. You, as the Creator's creation, are formed by it, through it, with it, and in it.

David was a king of Israel and one of humanity's greatest poets. His mind was in a headlock by deep depression and pendulum swings of emotion. He said of the Most High, *"If I go down to the place of death, you will be there"* (Psalm 139:8 ERV).

In every moment of your life, whether bedding in the depths or swinging in the heights, God has been with you. Even though it's a full-time job just dealing with the oxygen-free climate of deep despair, God is there as locksmith, key, and "open sesame" to all pathways of wholeness and joy. If someone has told you God will make your life even worse when coming to help you, Friend, that is a lie. It hurts because we hold on so tightly. It hurts because we want God to do our will for us. But Friend, God's pleasure is for your peace, joy, welfare, and fulfillment. Not just yours, but mine too. For all of ours.

Even if your lock is buried so far down you can't recall or maybe don't even know where it could possibly be, be loved, Beloved. Be loved.

82

THE KEY TO EVERY LOCK (PART 2)

Don't worry. Your Creator will find your lock for you. Your Creator knows where it is because you were made in benevolent and benign design. Here you are, utterly loved, utterly designed, utterly wanted, and ultimately—like the rest of creation—good, true, and beautiful. All that God made is.

Drop all those other keys, Friend. The keys engraved with the word "should" repeatedly. These expectations of others—some coax, some hoax—are where we need to tread softly. In that word *should* is the abode of the Father of Lies. It is where we keep the memory tapes of judgment and rejection, plus the "Measure Up!" measuring tapes from parents, family, friends, teachers, clergy, gurus, vibesters, and even strangers.

When God presents the key and opens the lock, there's no "should" about it. Simply, "Enter in, Friend. Enter into the joy of My love and desire for you." That desire is an end to a life of lockdown and deadlock, and the beginning of a no-holds-barred life of freedom and fulfillment. Worldly definitions of fame and fortune, fountains of youth, and finances need not apply. For above all that, in the eternal embrace of the everlasting arms, is so much more. Receive blockbuster blessings beyond anything you can fathom, much less contain or control. When you let God open your doors, you can't stop the love from flowing forth.

Trust God's heart and tell God your heart. Yes, pray, "Not my will, but Yours be done," but don't start there. (See Luke 22:42.)

Begin by asking God for what you will. Why shouldn't you share with God's heart "the desires of your heart"? (See Psalm 37:4.) God can handle whatever it is and wants to hear what's on your heart. Nothing is too small—or big—for the One who created you and cares for you. Hand God the ring of useless keys and be loved, Beloved. Be loved.

83

THE MAGNIFYING GLASS

Beloved, it isn't news to you that a magnifying glass makes whatever it is you're viewing larger. Sometimes this is good. For those with impaired vision, it makes reading possible. Words that are simply too tiny to make out need magnification, even by those with perfect sight. Engravers, diamond appraisers, and surgeons, to name a few, are people whose jobs require assistance by magnification.

In our lives, it's good to look at what we're trying to make larger and why.

These could be very real matters. Financial trouble, job difficulties, relationship strife, abuse, illness, death, and even things like car trouble and a home falling into disrepair can steal our focus and magnify themselves so we feel utterly helpless. Suddenly all we see are our problems.

Friend, you can stop the magnification that makes your trials, your tears, and your torments larger than life. There's no denying life can be difficult. Some days life feels like it's made to give us hardship. Add people into the mix, people with free will to love and hate, help or harm, to light the path or to create roadblocks. We wonder if this will be the way it is for the rest of our lives.

This despair is made larger when the difficulties of life are all we focus on.

Beloved, God will help you even here. God knows what your life is like. God knows your challenges, how you feel about things, and what you focus on. God knows you better than you know yourself. Your Creator, the One who loves you regardless of your comings and goings, will gladly give you eyes to see tomorrow. Do you understand, Dear One? God will give you a more clean and vigilant lens through which to view the light of creation and the lightbulbs of creativity. This magnifying glass spotlights the lightworks in the world around you, no matter how dark it seems right now.

All you have to do is ask God for a new lens, a lens of discernment and discreetness to replace the skewed and skewering magnification of all that is in the way of a life of joy.

When you ask God to give you Creator-Vision, life will open. It might seem a little hard at first to view others with the same love and compassion as our never-giving-up-on-love Creator. Even viewing ourselves this way can feel counterintuitive to so much of what we have been taught. The first step to change is honesty about where things currently are. In a collapse of illusion, look upon the ruins and remainders and say, "This is where I begin."

Let God have all of that. For only God knows how to turn even our mistakes and failures into something usable and good. Isn't that good news?

Magnify the good God has given you, Friend. The food you eat today. The air you breathe. The water you drink. The song you listen to most. Who is your friend? Can you call them? Make one change. Focus on one good thing today. Bring it to mind. Magnify it in meaning as something the True Light has given you to get through today.

More and more will reveal itself in the light of the Creator's goodness. God loves you, Friend. Ask for God's vision to see yourself and your situation with love and compassion. Let God be your lens. Let God lead.

Be loved, Beloved. Be loved.

84

THE STAR NURSERY

In the great Orion Nebula, a star nursery abides. Any lover of the skies can vouch for the mind-bending heat and winds that are everyday occurrences in the cosmos. Such forces would rip our planet apart. But instead, they are ripe for the creation of stars. Each star is wrapped in its own dusty blanket which, if astronomers are correct, will eventually coalesce into planets much like what happened when our Earth was forming.

In other words, Friend, the Creator has built purpose into the universe. If you're here, alive, receiving light, air, and water, God has a purpose for you. Living on this planet isn't always easy, as you know. God is not unaware of your plight. Quite the contrary. God is always with you and remembers everything you don't. The Creator is more aware than you are of all that you are. God has a blanket around you like the stars in the nursery of Orion. The blanket is God's love for you, Dear One.

This blanket not only surrounds you with compassion, comfort, healing, and hope, it will also help you grow. God's love will turn into meaning and purpose. When you emerge from the nursery of formation where winds are high and the heat seems almost unbearable, you will see worlds before your eyes:

Worlds of possibility.

Worlds of people.

Worlds of opportunity.

Worlds of grace.

Worlds of forgiveness.

Worlds of hope.

Worlds of love.

Worlds of creativity.

Worlds of meaning.

God's love, surrounding you like the swaddling of a child in the nursery, isn't wispy and full of whim. It can create all that you were created to receive, Friend. As much as God has plans for the stars in the nursery of Orion, God has hopes and dreams for you too. If God can create all that's necessary to form stars, how much more will God be able to create what we need to live a life of joy and meaning? The Maker of stars will blanket you with divine love and remake your life, Beloved. God's care is given to you day and night; it is God's joy. It is your right to receive it.

Did you hear that?

It is your God-ordained birthright to receive divine compassion and love, like a blanket, knowing God will form worlds before you to inhabit. When we receive God's compassion fully, we receive God's grace; and when we receive God's grace, we can receive God's strength.

This strength is always ready to heal, to uphold and support, and to help you today, tomorrow, and all the next tomorrows. The fact that stars are being formed tells us God is not finished with the universe, and God is not finished with you, Friend.

Pull the blanket of love around you, expect a world of God's making to form, and right now be loved, Beloved. Be loved.

85

EARS TO HEAR

If you're hearing these words, it isn't too late. If you're hearing these words, Beloved, it's because…you're alive. Despair has not won today! You are still here! You may be far away. But you're still here. Marvelously here. I'm *so* glad you are.

Here to hear. Here to hope. Here to think, feel, and act. Here to live, move, and breathe in your being. But more than all this, you are here to love—to love and be loved, with the full blessing of God with you every moment. Not only is God with you, but God has ears to hear as well.

God's ears hear everything. God's ears hear hearts. God hears your mind-sounds we call thoughts. God hears your mouth-sounds we call words. God hears your heart-sounds we call feelings. Sound is one of the great tells that there is life.

The baby cries when it enters the world, a wail erupting from newborn lips.

The wave crashes upon the shore, bringing in new bits of stone and shell, taking the old away with it.

Cars zoom by us with throaty openings of the throttle, and people spend big bucks to hear roaring sounds from HEMI engines.

Spatulas strike the side of pots and bowls.

Garments shush over our ears as we slide them over our heads.

God hears all of this too.

God hears you, Dear One. Not just your footfalls upon the creaky step, the rumble of your nervous stomach, or the words you speak. God hears your cries, your mournings, your groans, your stresses, even if you never make a sound. God hears all your heart-sounds.

Children playing hide-and-seek give up "sound clues" to be found, but the Maker of all hearts cannot help but hear all of our cries.

Divine ears are not just attuned to the vibration one thing makes when it strikes another or brushes against itself. God's ears are attuned to waves that issue from all that concerns us, all that over-whelms us, all that throws us into a place called despair. Despair feels like a vacuum, a place where nobody else follows us, a place where we reside as if abandoned, a place no ears welcome our cries.

Oh, Friend! We are never abandoned! We are never where God is not. God is everywhere, in all things, around all things, and through all things. From the highest star to the innermost burst of our being, God is.

God is. God is. God is.

None can run from God's presence or flee from God's love. In God, the lost are always found. In God nobody ever runs alone. When God made us in the divine image, God was saying, "I am always with you."

But why would God want to be here with us? "Why would God love me and want to help me?" some might ask. Perhaps you do too. We cringe and recoil, remembering the things we have done which have hurt others or led them down dead-end paths. "Surely, God is furious with me. Certainly, I deserve what I get. Because of my own actions, necessarily, God has turned away from me."

NO, No, no! God cannot turn away from you, Friend, or God would cease to be who God is. God loves you for who God is, not just for who you are. God is love. That love loved you into existence. That love wraps you tightly in this moment of your existence—right here, right now. God loves you despite the limits you would place on God, or on yourself. God loves you—whenever, whatever, and forever.

In the mind of God, you are memorized for all eternity. In the heart of God, you are cherished for all eternity. God hears your cries, sits with you in your despair, and is ready to help you in the best ways possible. Just honestly say, "Please help me. I need You."

When God hears your cries, it's not like an impatient parent who can't know all that you're feeling, all that you've been through and are going through. When God hears your cries, God knows exactly what you're feeling and everything you've been through. God says, "I am here. I love you. I know you. I will deliver you by my right hand of my righteousness."

God's righteousness. Not mine. Not yours. It's on God, who is more than willing to give divine righteousness *to* you, *for* you.

Friend, let God help you as only God can. Only God knows what is truly helpful. God loves you—not like a harsh teacher who makes things difficult. Things are already difficult. Let God listen, and love, and bear you up in the shelter of the everlasting arms. God knows what is best for what the Creator created.

Let God help you, Child of God, revealing the next step and the next. Hear the drumbeat of love from the God who hears you and be loved, Beloved. Be loved.

86

THE HAUNTED HOUSE

Have you ever gone to a haunted house with your friends around Halloween? While the gory and ghostly scenes are bad enough, the pitch-black corridors are the worst part, and if you get separated from the group, it can be downright terrifying.

Beloved, it seems almost natural to believe that when our life goes dark and isolated, God has wandered away. Like being trapped in the lightless corridors of a haunted house, we feel alone in the blackness for we cannot see in front of us, much less behind of us. We have no idea if someone is waiting to jump out and frighten us. We beg and plead for God to come back to us.

Believe it or not, Friend, God is often found in the darkness where you are. *"Moses went to the dark cloud where God was"* (Exodus 20:21 ERV). In other words, there is truly nothing to fear about where you are right now. Your Eternal Friend, like the haunted-house friend that finds you and sticks with you until you reach the door, is right with you. The Eternal Friend sees perfectly in the dark.

Darkness is as light to God. We misconceive that we control God's love. We believe that where we are is where we'll always be, that the dark night has come because the Light has deserted us.

How we imagine God to be can tell more about us and our story than about God and God's story. Perhaps it's always felt like a horror story. Perhaps we were introduced early on to a big-stick bully god waiting to jump out of the darkness and harm us. This prickly perfectionist god is unable to look upon us in our imperfections without harshly punishing our mischiefs and mistakes. Perhaps we were initiated into the cosmic concierge god. This "useful" god exists to accommodate our bidding and execute our plans. Yet when this god fails to do so, we're still somehow to blame. The blame-bringer and shame-monger whispers from the dark house's speakers, "It's your fault." Over and over.

God takes your hand. "So what if it is, Child? I'm here with you. We may have some more rooms to walk through in here, but I know where we're going. I see everything." And though you cannot see your Divine Friend, you feel God's touch, you hear God's voice. "May I escort you?"

Beloved, you can say "Yes!" to this invitation.

We have all "done what we ought not to have done, and not done what we ought to have done." We have all at times chosen not to love or be loving, not to forgive or be forgiving. We have all at times turned away from "godsends"—opportunities for aid and recovery and offers for friendship and compassion. To be in God's hands does not mean we will not walk through hard times or do bad things. But it does guarantee that those hands will not drop us or desert us or condemn us or slap us silly for doing wrong things.

Friend, this condemnation god, more like a feature in the haunted house than a helper, does not exist. For this god is a distortion, a stumbling block, an aberrant being controlled by the capricious whims and foibles of the very creation designed and constructed by the divine hand. Why would anybody serve a god like that? Why would anyone want to be close to a god like that, or trust in the care of a god like that? The God who made you, a masterwork of creation, is in for the distance. As the prophet Zephaniah once wrote, the God who made you *is in your midst...he will rejoice over you with gladness; he will quiet you by his love; he will exult over you with loud singing* (Zephaniah 3:17 ESV). God sings because of you.

Listen. Can you hear the love song over the speakers, right here in the darkness? "I made you. I love you. I am with you always."

Let God lead you through the house of darkness into the light and be loved, Beloved. Be loved.

87

NO PLACE TOO DEEP

Even with modern technology, humans have a challenging time finding sunken vessels and the treasures they contain. We use sonar. We look for comet tails of debris. Yet, searching for a sunken craft is much like trying to find a nail lying in a prairie—in the dark.

When life folds over us and we feel like it is submerging us, I want you to know, Friend, there is no depth in which you find yourself that God will not find you. Not only will God find you, but God will also stay with you. Not for the short run but for the long haul.

God already knows where you are and is already here.

In many ways, our griefs and losses feel so lonely only. No one else has lived your life or walked your "lonesome valley." Can you expect others to understand what has brought you to this dead-end where there seems to be no way forward? At times like this, we can feel so alone inside.

The truth is, God understands all this. Our God is "the compassionate and gracious God." Our Creator is imbued in all of creation. God's compassion feels what we feel, knows what we know and do not know, and experiences it firsthand along with us. God understands more than you, or I, or anyone can know. God's own description in the Old Testament is as follows: compassionate and gracious, slow to anger, abounding in love and faithfulness. (See Exodus 34:6.) There is no true compassion without the willingness to experience someone on their terms and suffer with them. God knows this better than anyone.

We live in a realm where the sum of humankind's choices is the landscape we see in any given moment. Sometimes "choice-and-consequences" leads us into deep waters. This is why the Creator deep dives into our deepest ocean. God knows there is a way out. The way out, Beloved, is up. God didn't create you to swim about blindly at the bottom of the sea, frightened that nothing will ever change. God redeems everything, even our suffering. But it is not the Creator that designs suffering for us, we who are so beloved to the Divine heart. It is not the One who loves eternally who says, "I will make you suffer unspeakable cruelties so I can comfort you with my love." This is psychopathic, and any parent who did this would be jailed. God isn't like that, Friend, though some have tried to make sense of suffering with such barbarous reasoning.

No one wishes anyone a difficult life. But sometimes it is the difficulties of life that bring out the artist in us and that birth our most beautiful thoughts and worthy deeds. This is trials turned to treasure, the treasure of who we are in light of how much God loves us. The treasure of placing our hand in the Creator's.

There is another realm that will lighten and enlighten you. It is the realm of spirit, the realm of the invisible, the realm of the heavenly. This realm isn't as separate as you might suspect. It can rip through space and time whenever one of God's children sends an SOS. God's infinite power and love will come to your aid, Friend. Only call out, "Help me." When you give God blanket permission over your life, miracles occur. That humble confession of neediness is the greatest self-help act you might ever do for yourself. But this self-help act is an abandonment of self-help: "Save me, for I can no longer save myself."

Surely, spiritual practices can help us help ourselves. But sometimes things have fallen so far apart that we have fallen too deeply into despair for even the most simple acts. We need God. We are needy people, all of us, and we were meant to need God. God honors our neediness. In such moments, God will shine most brightly as only God can. We weren't created to do it all ourselves so that we won't need God. The One who made you will deep dive to rescue and lift you up, scooping you into the everlasting arms. Receive that divine love, that holy aid, and be loved, Beloved. Be loved.

88

THE HOWL OF THE WOLF

When we cry out to God, Beloved, we can believe we are heard. We are heard right from where we are.

When a wolf becomes separated from its pack—which is the same thing that despair does to a human—it doesn't hunker down and wait to be found. It lifts its head and howls. A wolf in separation doesn't howl merely to express itself to itself. It howls so the pack might hear.

The pack is alerted to its member's loneness. The pack lifts their voices in return, and they cry back and forth to one another, each locating the other by the sound of the lone wolf's howl.

Cry to God, Friend. Lift your voice and cry out, "I am here, ready to be found."

All my shielding…
all my cocooning…
all my masking…
all my hiding…
all my self-isolating and self-loathing…
I'm done, God. I'm done.

Your cries are heard whether their sounds are horrifying or appalling or merely a whisper. They may repel others, but they compel God's lovingkindness. Like the pack of wolves, your cries will send divine love to find you right where you are. Rescue will occur, and in that reunion resides affirmation that you are never alone, no matter where you find yourself.

The Creator howls love in so many forms, such as through people who offer help—from a kind person at the grocery store, to your friend who is reading this to you, to others who are standing by waiting for you to receive them. Perhaps you have family members who will gladly step in and uphold you, who will help you when you finally cry, "I'm ready to be heard. I'm even ready to receive the new that will sweep out the old."

Sometimes our cries bring with them a set of instructions. But, Friend, if we all knew exactly how to get ourselves up and out of the tar pits and pitch lakes, we wouldn't still find ourselves there. Cry to God, Beloved. Cry, "Help me," and then let yourself be found, cleansed in healing love, and delivered back to wholeness. Your willingness to recognize the God who is our help in time of trouble, and to trust the deliverance God sends, will amplify the cry of the divine voice assuring you that our best help comes from the Lord. Lift up your voice and hear God echo back, "Be loved, Beloved. Be loved."

89

LOOK UPON YOUR HAND

Do you see your hand, Friend? Have you noticed the fine articulations of your fingers where they bend and straighten? Do you see the tendons on the back of your hand? They tighten and loosen, enabling you to let go. Your hands facilitate most of the necessary tasks for survival, for enjoyment, and for service.

Your hands are a gift and a sign from your Creator. Ponder that for a moment. God equipped you with built-in tools capable of the finest precision movement of a master artist or skilled mechanic. You are no stranger to that. Even putting toothpaste on a toothbrush or writing your signature requires that kind of skill.

Our hands give. Your hands were made to give. To prepare food, caress those you love, hold a baby so its head doesn't flop. To grip the handle of a lawnmower. To push the buttons on a washer and dryer. To swirl a bristle brush around the commode. We give all the time.

Giving is what the Creator made us to do and be. God's own self is "giving." Given is what all things are, and gift is who you are. You are a gift. In fact, some of the greatest thinkers of all time, when trying to come up with a "proper name" for the third way of confessing the holy mystery of God, whittled the candidates down to one: Gift. When we cease to open our hands in giving, we lose part of who we are. We were meant to be a part of the life of abundant giving, that is, the very being of God.

Did you know you were meant to be here right now and your hands are living proof? God would not have equipped you with such magnificent tools if you were not fully capable of using them to participate in creation. Oh, Dear One, we are all crying out to one another for help in one way or another. We need you. You are a vital part of the gift of humanity.

But our hands are not just one-way tools. Our hands were made to receive too. In fact, that's what we do in order to give. Who is the giver of the greatest gifts? Who longs to place good things in your hands, not just to give to others but also to sustain the one God loves and cherishes (you!) and has willed into existence?

Your marvelous Creator!

Have you been wondering what to do with your hands? Do you stare at them? Do you wonder what will happen if you stop sitting on them? Do you feel as if they are tied?

Know this, if you're willing, God will place into your hands more than you can hold. This is why: you are meant to love just as much as you are meant to be loved. God will love you with abandon—abundantly, unquestioningly, utterly—so you can become love's conduit, a channel, a crucible, and a cup of blessing.

To be blessed, your hands receive.

To be a blessing, your hands give.

This circle of life will heal. This way of God will bring order out of chaos, restoring your hands, the miraculous tool that they are, to be reinstated in giving that enables meaning, joy, and wonder. Your giving becomes the receiving, your acts of service a reception of who you were truly meant to be—a grand, generous, and glorious lover of the creation and the Creator.

Friend, receive the love of the One who made you, who made me, who made all of us in God's glorious image. What else around you has been bequeathed to you that you no longer use? Is there something you take for granted that would better serve another?

Start now. Use your God-given tools to receive, to give, to let yourself know "I'm here" and why "I'm here."

"Yes, I can still serve. I'm worthy to pass the love along."

Knowing you can pass along the love, be loved, Beloved. Be loved.

90

THROWING CRATES OVERBOARD

We've all heard the stories of ships being buffeted at sea in a howling squall. Sailors trim the sails, lash up their lifelines, and batten down the hatches leading into the belly of the vessel. In the worst of storms, they throw cargo overboard to lighten the vessel, to keep its waterline higher and the ship less likely to be overtaken by the waves.

Friend, your waterline might be deeper than you ever bargained for. Loss, change, even the revealing of a truth you never asked for can weigh down your ship in the storms of life.

More likely than not, there are people and responsibilities, loss and insufficiencies, that weigh us down so greatly we wonder how we're still breathing. Perhaps you have found yourself in this situation and wonder, "Will this ever end?" Unlike the sailors throwing excess cargo overboard, there are some matters, some people, in your life you cannot do that to. We have to work. We have to put one foot in front of the other, no matter how difficult it seems, and it feels like we're about to drown.

Oh, Friend! No! You don't have to drown! That is not what you were created for when the Creator dreamed up the beautiful, holy being you truly are. God saw you sailing on the vessel of the Creator's design, light and nimble, in perfect union with God's intended journey for you.

Fear. Helplessness. Resentment. Unforgiveness. Shame. Blame. Grievance. Jealousy. Rage. These are all crates that cannot only be thrown off your boat but are longing to be hoisted overboard! They don't belong with you. They don't belong to anyone, really. You were made to be free. God hurls your harms and hurts into the deep blue sea where they sink like stones. Such gestures of grace cause us to wonder, "Who is a God like you?"

Don't go dredging up what God has already cast asunder. Did you hear that? God has already cast all that away within God's eternal love and knowing.

What can you throw overboard too, Friend? The good news is, God will reveal to you what is most besetting to you. God will help you cast aside notions that weigh you down. All the "if only" and "why me" helplessness can be placed in God's hands as "What's done is done. I'm ready to move on." Can it really be that simple?

Yes.

Is it hard to do that?

Yes, it is. Letting go is never easy. We not only have such toxic cargo with us but in many ways we have used it as comfort, as bricks in castle walls so we can feel safe inside. We grip our hands around such things. Releasing such a powerful grasp takes grit and gumption. Dear One, God will be that grit, that gumption. God will do it all with gusto.

Asking God to tag that which is weighing you down, that which pushes you below the waterline of freedom, is the first step. The second is using the light of truth to locate the hidden crates you claimed as yours that were never meant to be.

God will help you cast them over the side if you stop protecting them. Your vessel will be free to move through the storms, the calm seas, and everything in between. Because what is also true is this: the same divine hand that helped you throw bad ballast overboard will join your hand upon the tiller.

All along the ways and the waves, God will help you, revealing shorelines made for your pleasure and ports that will bring you peace.

With God, your vessel moving in its good design, your journey is assured.

Be loved, Beloved. Be loved.

91

THE HORIZON IS CLOSER THAN
YOU THINK

It's so easy to look for the light over the horizon, isn't it? We watch it for the rising of the sun, the blowing in of a storm, the arrival of visiting guests, or family coming home. We cast our gaze to the farthest point we can see and sometimes await rescue, our hope pinned on the distant future or something unexpected arriving just in time.

Friend, the horizon is closer than you think. You see, we can only abide where we are in this place, in this body, and at this moment. God knows this. God knows that here on earth we see the present in limitation, the future remains dim, and we are prone to view the horizon as the place from whence our deliverance comes.

Breathe for a moment, would you?

Inhale. Exhale. Inhale again.

Now look around you—right here, right now. See what has arrived in times past to provide for you, to comfort you, to give you truth, beauty, and goodness. Perhaps it's the gift of a friend who has been trying to reach out to you for some time. Perhaps it's a book or a quote that arrived just when you needed it.

Open your eyes just for a moment, this moment, Dear One. See what God has already brought to you. Check your messages and see who has reached out. Look in your refrigerator. Remember the delivery person who laid your pizza outside your door.

Then...go in deeper, Beloved. Because there's a horizon—your horizon—where God remains inside, never just on the other side of the hill or beyond those trees. God is never out of sight because you are never beyond the sight of the One who sees you, the One who knows you, the One who made you, the One who cares for you, for me, for everybody.

There's no such thing as a horizon with God. Live inside the eternal boundaries of what you can truly know, what you are able to experience with God, Dear One. The mystery beyond, the potential, the infinite possibilities can be taken from your stress-filled thoughts and given to the Creator's safekeeping. What will come can be from the hand of your giving and forgiving God. The Most High knows the end from the beginning and will bring to you what is most suited to your healing and growth.

Look around you, Friend. Where has God shown up? Look within you. Where is God now? With you always! Found deep inside, in the image of the Creator, where who you truly are and were made to be is fully present. There abides your First Love, the One who not only is with you but can and will bring you out of your pit of disappointment, decay, and despair, if you but place your hand in the hand of your Creator.

A little risk is all it takes. The barest, feeblest whisper of "Yes."

Risk the trust and patience of waiting and seeing what God brings you. No horizon necessary. Only Presence, and Presence that brings life, healing, passion, and hope. Hope in God, Friend. Not what's "happening" over the horizon.

God is with you here. Now. The everlasting arms are ready, eager, and able to engage for you, to stand with you, to help you stop waging a secret (or street) fight with life, to hold you from now into eternity.

Be loved, Beloved. Be loved.

92

STAY WITH US

Stay with us, God, when the storms of life are strong and the sea feels as if it is trying to oust us from our ship.

Stay with us, God, when light turns to lightning or the sun shines too brightly, blinding us with heat and rage.

Stay with us, God, when life seeks to explode within us in ways that destroy our peace and singe anything good we try to do.

Stay with us, God, when the night is dark and far spent and the only thing we know for sure is the hammering of our heart and the breath that is going in and coming out.

Stay with us, God, when the cold is so very cold and all before us seems immobile, locked in the ice of inertia, confusion, and an inability to remember the sunny climate we know can live within our heart.

Stay with us, God.

God will! God will stay with you, me, all of us, through all the weather that life drops down in various portions, at various places, and in various times and circumstances.

The sky of our existence is not always sunny and blue. Sometimes the heavens will open and display their glory. There will be cloudy days and storms. There will be rainy days and drizzling. There will be snowy days and blizzards. There will be gully washers that turn into twisters and hurricanes. God stays with us, whatever the weather. But there will be rainbows; the skies will always clear.

Whether or not we can see the atmosphere of life as good, lifting us up and swaddling us in its sway and swath, God still stays with us.

Whether or not we choose the shadows, refusing to face what is lacking in our life, our fake beliefs about ourselves and others, or our baked-in beliefs about a god who makes us cower in fear or alternatively takes a knee to our whims, God still stays with us.

Whether or not the cold seeps so deep inside of us that the despair, disappointment, and disillusionment become a craggy bedrock of hopelessness, God still stays with us.

God stays with you, Friend. Still. No matter what you do or say or think or feel. No matter how tangled and bungled your relationships. God still stays with you.

It isn't logical to believe in a creator that turns back from its creation, but many of us were taught just that.

Here's what is true.

You are formed from God, by God, in God, and for God. God is everywhere. God is All in All, and God stays. Even when we shun God's benevolent power by believing more in the omnipresence of evil than the omnipresence of God's goodness, God still stays with us.

No matter the storm, no matter the heat, the humidity, or the cold, God has not abandoned you. To abandon you, the Most High would have to abandon the very being in which you, me, and all of us live, move, and have *our* being.

Knowing God always stays, knowing that God's stillness will help you be still in one peace, allow your Creator's healing stillness and enduring presence, and be loved, Beloved. Be loved.

93

PASSPORT TO ANOTHER LAND

There's so much that awaits you beyond this change-resistant place where you live now, this oxygen-deprived space where light feels as if it comes only in slivers and glimpses. You need so much more than that to find your way or to find your passion for living.

We hold in our minds the idea of a land that we think, and sometimes feel, will hold all of life's answers. This hallowed ground will meet all our needs. We see its borders before us, a land of plenty, a place of sweetness and love. It seems rimmed by mountainous borders, by crags and cliff faces that are impossible to climb. We've been inspired by bravehearted accounts, both spiritual and physical, from people who love to climb and have boasted the strength to hoist the rope and pull themselves upward. Perhaps we've even tried their advice and seemingly failed. But all that seems impossible right now, doesn't it?

Perhaps you know you're not there right now. Perhaps even getting out of bed to brush your teeth feels like a monumental mission. Despair and depression bring on a pain of their own that those fortunate enough not to be dragged down into their vertigo cannot understand. "Pull up on your bootstraps! You've got this!" they cry with unintended cruelty. And you might, if you had the strength, answer, "Was there a boot camp for bootstrapping? I must have missed it. Besides, see any boots? I've been barefooted for a long time."

The land is so elusive. If only there was a passport for an easier entry.

Friend, there's a passport in your hand. This is the passport you've been looking at for years, the one that others have placed there after filling it out for you. Well-intentioned parents, pastors, teachers, politicians, celebrities, gurus, and self-helpers.

Many of these folks hold forth what seems to be hopeful advice. But none of these people are here with you, are they? Right here. Right now.

Friend, that passport given to you by the government of family and friends is to a country that isn't your native home. Your native land isn't like anybody else's. Trying to get there is like trying to get anywhere with a fake passport. Your country is your life. Your real passport is being held out for you to take, held in the hand of the One who loves you unconditionally. All you need to do to take it is turn around. Turn away from the impossible peaks and the plummeting valleys, the cold and ragged winds. Receive the passport to another land on which is engraved in gold the word "Love." The place God invites you to call your home is where love and joy rule the roost. We all know this world has challenges. But you never have to be alone, wandering a pathless journey, rappelling downward into the darkness. Beloved, even the darkness is not dark to God. In God there is light, and that light is your life, your very energy, your spirit, the baseline of who you are.

Receive the passport you were given when you were born to a commonwealth called Love. Only God knows exactly the steps that get you there perfectly. The One who knows you inside-out will direct your paths. This land doesn't arrive all at once. But each day a signpost will appear. Each day love will manifest in some form to light the next step. Be open to receive it. Be open to opportunities to share that love with others, for in the giving is a receiving that is truly divine. With every step, God will accompany you to the land that doesn't require a passport at all. Beside you is the One who says, "They're with Me." And that is enough.

Be loved, Beloved. Be loved.

94

ONE LIGHT, ONE LOVE, MORE THAN ONE GOOD NIGHT'S SLEEP

Truly, only One Light, One Love exists. There is One God. That One God is light, and in that light there is no darkness at all. God is love, and no love exists apart from God. Yes, duskiness can enfold us. Yes, lovelessness assaults us in so many ways, shapes, and forms. No wonder we can't get a good night's sleep.

Because God is much more mighty to save than anything malicious is to harm, we can actually sleep. Because the reigning and resting state of the All in All is bright and pure and holy, you can put your head on that pillow without worrying about your problems. Whatever your situation is, the One who created the whole universe is big enough to help you through your valleys, over your hills, and carry your baggage so you can sleep all night. *In peace I will both lie down and sleep; for you alone, O LORD, make me dwell in safety"* (Psalm 4:8 ESV).

There is, of course, a basic reason why we fall short on slumber: we usually have something on our mind. But inside each one of us— you, me, and all beings—resides the One Light, the One Love, that can help us lay aside the rest so we can rest. Let that Light surround you and that Love infill you so that you can sleep peacefully, free of whatever has bound you. Let the arms of God enfold you so you can lay down and put down all the tormenting pain and torturous thoughts that rob your rest.

Even now, in your fitful slumber, One Light, One Love is with you, in you, and abiding over you. Of course, it is your right as a free will being to choose to focus on what has already happened in your life if you let it: the rejection, the fallenness, the fear, and the confusion. But we have a truth locked deep within us, ready to drive away the desperation, love away the hate, lullaby to sleep the anxiety, and clear up all the confusion. That truth is the light and love of your Creator, the One who knows, the One who knows you, the One who yearns for your communion and love.

Receive the light and love of God as the default setting of your days and nights. Take for granted that God cares for you rather than believing you must earn that parental favor and goodness. God loves you as a child because you are God's child. And every good parent lays their child down to rest in peace, safety, and quiet.

Perhaps it's easier to believe in that love for others, but not for yourself. Many of us are far more capable of saying "God loves you" than "God loves me." But this love is not external, Friend, it shines from within. What is more, it is always shining. This One Light, One Love,

is the brick and mortar of all you are and all you are meant to build in this lifetime.

Ask God right now, "Just tonight, will You care for my cares? Help those I can't?" See the light, feel the love, dream in peace. Know this is the truth. This is the true place from which all springs forth to you and might spring forth from where you are, day after day, night after night.

Know God loves you. Let God's light illumine each day and night, one after the other. Trust the Creator's goodness and ability to light your path, lighten your load, and lighthouse you safely back to yourself.

Sleep well, Friend, and be loved, Beloved. Be loved.

95

BEHIND THE BLINDS

Imagine homeowners who move into a new home bought sight unseen. They call the realtor. "We don't understand why it is night here, even during the day!"

The realtor scratches her head. "I don't understand. What's going on?"

"We walk outside sometimes during the day, and it's sunny, but as soon as we go back inside, it's pitch black."

The realtor responds, "This is such a mystery. I mean, I knew those blinds and blackout curtains were good ones, but—"

The homeowner interrupts, "Blackout curtains? Blinds? Nobody told us about any blinds."

While it seems silly, it would be even less sensible if the homeowner called back a few weeks later with the same problem.

The truth is, what keeps the sun from shining is not about our house, our windows, or even our curtains. The sun will shine regardless. But we can pull down the blinds, shut the blackout curtains, turn our backs, close our eyes, and the effects will feel just the same. We will be in darkness, not of God's making, but of our own.

Dear One, God's love is always radiating from the heart of the heavens. God doesn't turn away from you, for how can the One who made you do so? If the old saying is true that there is no person you would not love if you only knew their story, how much more true is that of God, who knows every twist and turn, every jot and tittle of your story?

Yes, there is a phenomenon called the *dark night of the soul*. But these "dark nights" can be your invitation to know God better, discover God within, and put the sky back in your soul.

Life's greatest awakenings can happen at the depths of our darkness if we keep our eyes open. The One who loves you even when you don't love yourself is ready to reveal the Light that is for you alone, that is your very life, your beeline between you and the Source of all you are. One on one. Blessed Creator to the beloved creation.

If you feel like you can't open the blinds, Friend, ask God to help you. God will show you what are enlightenments and what are "endarkenments" and how they sometimes masquerade as each other. God will remove the thick window coverings and turn you around to face the Light. In fact, God delights in doing so. Like the good friend God is, God will not blast the Light upon you in blinding force all at once. Each day, little by little, your life will warm to God's tender touch, mending embrace, and unfailing kindness.

In Judaism, the day begins at sundown. Candles are lit on Friday night to begin the Sabbath. Your own resurrection can begin in this dark night. Even this place can now become the birthplace of new life and new creation. The God found in your darkness is revealed by light. Just ask the butterfly.

And guess what? God's light is here...right now!

Invite in the light of your Creator. Raise the blinds. Walk in the Light as the light-footed creature God made you to be. Walk in the Light as God is in the Light. God is Light. Face the unfailing love and unflinching light of God, and be loved, Beloved. Be loved.

96

THE SPIRAL STAIRCASE

Life is sometimes referred to as an uphill climb. It's easy to picture a staircase to go along with that. It would be nice, wouldn't it, if we could see the top step? For if we could, we might better figure out the choices we should make on all the treads in between. But life isn't like that. We think we know what tomorrow will bring, but the hard truth that anything can happen is part of the human lot. You know that as well as anyone.

When using a staircase to describe our life's journey, perhaps a spiral staircase would suit us better. We can see the next step, maybe a few, but for every step that is revealed, there is another new step that remains hidden, around the curve and out of sight. The good news, Beloved, is that God knows what's on every single step and what is waiting at the top.

What is waiting, you might ask?

Peace, joy, and love. These are what God, the One who made you and loves you and cares for you, has planned for every single one of the Creator's children. At the top of this staircase is your loving reunion with the Creator. God is patient, not wanting anyone to perish, including you. (See 2 Peter 3:9.)

But your Creator is also the One who is with you always. God is on the very same step you are on right now. God will not only climb with you, but your Creator will also meet you on the next step too. There is no place you can walk where God is not, no place you can go where God will not meet you. You cannot be so ground down that the Ground of Being will not gather you up and get you better.

You can go up or down on this staircase, and still, God will be with you. For God is everywhere. But, Beloved, God's desire for you is to lead you upwards toward a life where you walk in trust, knowing that each day comes for your benefit, for your growth, for your goodness. Because God is good.

Place your hand in the hand of the One who loves you with a never-giving-up love. Take the next step with God in trust that the day will bring to you a way of rescue, a way through every trough of despair, a way in which deliverance comes in ways you cannot predict. The One who made the universe is not at a lack to know what to do. The One who made you is not at a lack to know how to do it. The One who made all things is not lacking the power to accomplish all the divine hand sets out to accomplish. God is love. Step by step, God's love will find a way. God's love will reach the top. Love is already there.

Knowing this, be loved, Beloved. Be loved.

97

A LOVER TO BE EMBRACED

For a while, this bumper sticker was popular: Life Sucks, Then You Die. Yikes! It's so easy to view this planet as a combat zone, and other humans—even ourselves—as an enemy to be battled, a field to be conquered. We stake our claims in flood zones, agree to lifelong relationships with abusers, ingest harmful substances, and adhere to loveless lies. We find ourselves wallowing in the shame and blame of perfectionistic expectations for ourselves and others. In many ways, we can become our own worst enemies. When we do, everything around us appears much the same.

What if we saw our lives as something less reflexively reactive and a little more proactively loving? What if we put this phrase on our cars instead: Life Is Beautiful, So Love It While You're Here.

If existence is a battle to be fought, a war to be won, a mess to be cleaned up, or a problem to be overcome, no wonder we meet each day in fear, exhaustion, and despair. No wonder life is a wonderland no longer. Life becomes Malice in Wonderland.

Who really wants to live there?

God can change that for you, Dear One, through one simple word: love. And in one simple way for you to begin seeing the world differently: receive. God needs only one word from you in order to love you in ways large and small, from the rising to the setting of the sun, and that word is "Yes."

Like any good lover requires, assent must be given. It is your freedom and right to allow God to love you or not. It doesn't matter why we refuse the best and kind affections of our Creator; God will respect our boundaries. God will not enter your house if you say "No." God stands at the door and knocks (see Revelation 3:20). The

Creator will not turn your resting place into love if you refuse to let God in. Forced affection isn't affection at all.

But see the rose, Friend. Revel in its ravishing aroma. Relish the goodness of your food. Sense the oxygen being taken into your lungs as breath. Be loved by the world, and by the God who makes all things new. The good things around you are here for your enjoyment. They are here as love tokens from the One who is the greatest lover the world has ever known.

Be loved by the beauty of the planet and the bounty of its Creator. Instead of all of your fears pushing away the good things of life, delight in them. Love God as the lover who loves you eternally, infinitely, and without regard to anything you have done or ever will do. God's love is a walk-a-thousand-miles love.

Walk in that love. Step by step. Yes by yes. Moment by moment. In God be loved, Beloved. Be loved.

98

THE PARK BENCH

God's already waiting for you on the park bench, Beloved. As you wander the path that is your life, rest stops pop up along the way. Many times we view those as places we invite God to join us, and indeed, God will. God doesn't need you to be perfect to deserve the Divine Presence or to earn it in any way, shape, or form. Because the Creator is always ready to attend God's child—and you are God's child.

But Friend, there is a park bench where God already sits, awaiting your arrival and beckoning you come. It sits just at the edge of who you think you are, who you deem others to be, and where you think you abide. God sits waiting in the impossible made possible, the dim made bright, the booby traps made harmless, the emptiness made full.

On God's park bench is a place just for you, the invitation engraved in eternity, manifested in time and space, just beyond anything you ever expected. Your eye hasn't seen, Friend, nor has your ear heard anything the likes of what God longs to prepare for you if you will just come to the bench and make time for your Creator. Sit down here, scoot closer, lay your burdens down, put up your feet, rest your head upon the shoulder of the Living Rock, and sigh, "I'm ready."

Ready to be loved. Ready to be cared for. Ready to behold the parting of seas, the calming of storms, the way made straight in full knowledge of all you are, all you have been through, and all you were initially created to be.

The park bench upon which God sits only asks for you to trust. For, Dear One, this bench isn't stationary. This bench isn't where you watch the world go by, leaving you in its dust or drowning you in its wake. This bench is a chariot of hope, faith, and love. This bench is the forward movement of God beneath you—God in command because God knows best. God sees the end from the beginning. God wants to love you perfectly.

Sit down, won't you? Allow yourself to rest. Trust in the One who made you, me, and all of us. Let yourself say "Yes" to God. "Yes" to God's love. "Yes" to God's peace. "Yes" to God's design for your life.

Each day is all that is required. No drafting a five-year plan. No shaking a Magic 8 Ball. No gazing into any crystal ball. No blueprint to template and trace. Because you've placed yourself in God's embrace, trust the Be-All and End-All to strengthen you for whatever life brings. God will prepare you to go with guts and gusto through parklands, forests, and mountain trails you never knew existed.

Sit down with God, Friend, and be loved, Beloved. Be loved.

99

THE TREES TELL THE TALE

Friend, I invite you to walk with me along a pebbled path. The springtime trees grow from dark and fertile earth, out of vibrant, new green grass. The earth is rejuvenating. Winter fades in patches of old snow best left to melt. Decaying leaves and decomposing twigs return to loam and humus. The park is beautiful today. Fruit trees spire in various stages. There are pears in white bloom. The cherry trees hold their budded blossoms close within the protection of pointed green leaves. We meander around boulders. We cross over rushing creeks full of melted ice and snow.

This park has seen the seasons come and go for many years now. The leaves tell the story. Tender green, it must be spring. Dark and slick, the mature greens of summer are displayed. The riotous russets of autumn showcase shades of bronze and gold and flaming red. The bare, woody branches rest in winter. By the trees we know the season in which we stand. By the path we know where we stand.

Sometimes, Dear One, it helps to know where we are on the path of life. Seasons enter and exit as they do, bringing cold and heat, light and dark, camouflage or conspicuousness. But through each season your path remains, the place you set your feet, the place you move them and bring them to rest again.

Beloved, no matter the season, God is present with you on your path. It is true that our choices, even circumstances beyond our control, propel us down various meandering trails. But you can make each step count for something and toward something—a life of meaning, a life of hope, a life of peace and joy. A life brimming with excitement, wide-eyed wonder, and an existence that will catch your breath. A place of dreaming, a place of movement that is trusting, steady, and laid out before you by the Pathfinder and Way Maker.

Take the path of trust in the One who made you, the One who loves you, the One who knows you better than you know yourself, and the One who finds beauty in your uniqueness.

Each day is made to be an advent and adventure. Each day can be the day we decide to let God plant our steps, bloom before us, blossom within us, leaf out around us, and expose the architecture that supports us. Step by step, Friend, is the way it works. Like a stream in the desert, each day delivers its provisions for the journey. Each day renders itself perfect for who you are and who you were made to be.

Ask the Creator to direct you and help you receive what is waiting for you at this step on the path, in this season, and the next, and the next, and in each one, be loved, Beloved. Be loved.

100

SHARDS OF TRUTH

Are you shattered? Are you scattered? Are you unable to find your footing in a world that feels unstable and mean-spirited? Are you eaten up by "reality"? The news we read, the hostilities we hear, the hatred we feel, the fights we flee or engage in—all affect our perception of reality.

We tend to define ourselves by our disappointments, our resentments, our failures. We tend to remake ourselves in response to the worst within us and among us, which can bring out the worst from us. Reframing around the worst, not the best, can also trip us into pits of despondence and despair. You are not the first to say to God, whether silently or screaming, "Why was I even born?" Job, a prophet both to Judaism and Islam, did so during his period of extreme suffering.

The more we amass weaponry to protect our inner selves against the wiles of the world, the more we shoot ourselves in the foot. The more we try to fit into an unruly world riven with strife and struggle, especially in ways seeking to bring meaning and joy, the more we sink to the bottom of ourselves. Broken for trying. Broken for believing in the wrong people and the wrong gods. Broken in our sunken hopes and abandoned dreams. We see our ego-constructed self around us in pieces. We have no idea how to even begin picking through them.

Friend, there is good news in this chaos, a message in the mess. For in those pieces are found what is false: our injured responses to unachieved expectations, our ragged illusions about life, the downright lies we believe and tell ourselves. Those pieces can now be cast away.

As you sit among the shards, ask God to sit with you, to help you, and to reveal what is truly part of you and what was put there by other people and other means. There are parts of you which have never been who you truly are. But the better news is that there are sacred parts of you that are meant to be rediscovered. God will hold you in divine care while removing parts that aren't who you truly are and restoring that which needs mending. The Creator will make of you an old-new creation, presenting you with pieces you had no idea existed much less noticed in the fallout.

All in perfect timing.

The truth is, the Creator sees you as part of the "it-is-good" spoken into existence from the very start of time. That cannot and will not change. What God creates, God creates for good and for the forevermore. You are part of the goodness of God. You are part of the beauty of God. You are part of the truth of God. Allow the One who knows you to reassemble the breakage of your life.

You are a priceless vessel made to receive the outpouring and overflowing love of God. God can glue your broken pieces back together with gilded salves and lacquers of love. Even the cracks left behind, if repaired with grace and mercy, hold new beauty. In every life story there can be found meaning in the marring. True wholeness takes all your story into an accounting, a totality of your comings, shortcomings, and overcomings; your wheat and weeds; your falling-downs and falling-outs. The scars, stretch marks, and seams are life's beauty marks. You might call your wounds windows to the grace that overwhelms guilt and calms your grief. They can become torchlights for your path, and the light of understanding on others' paths of growth and greatness.

This is what's coming, Friend. This is your birthright. Wellness is what was meant to be. You. In wholeness. In totality. Every tear a tale, every anguish a badge of honor, every torment taken into consideration—to be used as a balm in the healing of yourself and others.

The shattered vessel becomes whole and strong again. Not by hiding the cracks or covering up the imperfections, but by filling the fractures with the stardust of the universe and the gold dust of the earth out of which you were made by the hand of God.

And then, be filled with the light of the Good Creator, and be loved, Beloved. Be loved.

101

A SEED BY ALL MEANS

A seed by all means seems to be a dried up, lifeless thing. It's easy to crush a seed under our heel and render it useless. Indeed, left in a dry envelope with other seeds, it isn't much better. The potential is there, yes. But left on its own, with others in the same state, nothing new coming in or going out, is it any wonder it stays just as it is?

It's so easy to fall into a place where life feels dry, hard, and without hope. We get tucked into envelopes of despair and despondency, stuffed in these dark and dry places. We even find ourselves with others in the same situation. So we resign ourselves to a life that doesn't seem like it will ever sprout green and tender, full of new life, flowers, and food.

The good news is that within the seed that you are, no matter what, is contained the DNA design of what you were made to be! God didn't make us to be stored away in envelopes and forgotten. Or stacked on shelves of potting sheds to be pulled out at the Creator's whim.

God made you to be planted in good, healthy soil. Sometimes it's hard to see when you're first planted, yes. But know that there's heat and nutrients in the soil of God. When the water of the Spirit, the One that gives life, finds its way down to you, the hard shell is softened, and you will begin to stretch, to sprout, and to break free!

God will plant you in the garden of the Creator's care so that you can live a life of love, an abundant love at that. In the garden you will break through the surface of the soil and reach to the heavens, even as you grow deep roots in God's beautiful creation.

Call upon God. "Save me from being buried alive. Rescue me from this dry and weary casket of paper and print, oh, Creator! Water me with Your Spirit. Refresh and renew me. Nurse me in your garden nursery and bring me to life."

Friend, God will place you in the kind of soil in which you were meant to thrive. God will root you and fertilize you with loving care, helping you grow into all you were meant to be. But let God do the tending, Friend. It's always best. The Master Gardener knows the right amount of sun, the right amount of rain, the right amount of shade. Even the pruning, when done by the Creator, removes that which is dead, not that which is alive and truly pleasing not just to God but to you too.

Be who you are, rooted and grounded in the Creator's garden. Growing to maturity. Strong in your setting. Tended and nurtured by the skilled hand of the Master Gardener, be loved, Beloved. Be loved.

102

A NEW WELL

There is a well of living water, Friend, a well from which you are invited to drink every single day. It is the well of God's wellness for you. Your Eternal Parent created you with wellness and wholeness in mind, just as your earthly parents birthed you with the same dreams for your life. Yes, the world does hold its share of challenges for humanity. We solve problems that create more problems to solve. Our cures for diseases create more diseases to cure.

On the home front, if it isn't curdling relationships, financial circumstances, or societal hardships, nature provides us with ample opportunities to buckle under her volcanoes, viruses, twisters, and tsunamis. Believing we are ill-equipped for our own lives, and not seeing how we can ever be, is the number one well-blocker and one of the things at the heart of despair. Oh, but Friend...

Draw close to the well. God musters us, the Creator's flock, to a well from which we might drink. In drinking the Living Water, we receive life. The well of God's love is the place where you can drink without looking over your shoulder for predators. The well of God's affection doesn't sweep you under because it is a still well. God leads you beside still waters, to restore and re-story your soul (see Psalm 23). All you have to do is drink.

At this well, your well that is put before you each day, not only will you find everlasting love but God will also hold you in the everlasting arms while you drink in that love. Peace is found in the everlasting arms. But it's not peace as the world gives, Friend. It's the peace that can't be understood (see Philippians 4:7). That kind of peace doesn't require perfect circumstances or perfect people around you. It doesn't even require you to be perfect. All it requires is for you to say, "Yes, I will drink." For while you are at the well, you can realize the perfect safety of your true and eternal self, the inner being that recognizes itself in the love of its Creator.

At the well, you might look down at your own reflection and see yourself as your Creator sees you. Made by God, fashioned in divine love, you are part of all that God made. You are a reflection of all that God proclaimed, "It is good," even before time began. God knew God would create. God knew what God would create. God knew you were part of that creation. Look upon your beautiful reflection in the water and see, and know, that you are made by God, just as you are. Earth has nothing to show more fair than you.

The Living Water of love will flow into all the places you once thought were impossible to find. God knows your deepest, most hidden secrets and still loves you and desires your presence. You were made to be loved, Friend. You were made to drink freely from this well. Drink all you want, Friend. There's always more where that came from!

Drink, Child of God, and allow the water to permeate and saturate you to overflowing today. Invite in the light of the love you were made to receive in all its beauty and glory. Allow it to flow into you. Today, give yourself to watching what it does, and every day thereafter. You see, your Creator knows exactly what you need in advance. Out of that "inner spring welling up to eternal life" (see John 4:14) is what you, me, and all of God's children need. For the rehydration of your soul, be loved, Beloved. Be loved.

103

A HEALING BALM

Friend, God longs to heal you. Your pain and suffering matter to the One who loves you without measure.

There is nothing that puts us in our place, and pops the balloon of our pride and independence, like sickness, pain, irrevocable loss, and suffering.

There are two kinds of pain: hurt pain that signifies sickness and danger, and healing pain that registers recovery and health. The one requires engagement and treatment. The other requires endurance and trust. Both require prayer and community—and God.

God is in the healing—not the hurting—business.

Know that God cares when you've tried and failed. That's when the Creator yearns to be nearest to show you how much God cares. God's deliverance is for all who desire to be rescued. Our trust is in God, not the power of the sword, the glitter of money, the grandeur of fame, the glory of our own intellect, or the subtle allure of transactional deeds of service. A culture of "things" rips off our wallets even as it rips apart our hearts. Besides, who has more power, wealth, and wisdom than God?

Beloved, God's healing balm is never expressed in punishment raining down from heaven. That is the balm that embalms. For the true balm of heaven to work, all it takes is for your wounded spirit to say, "Yes, heal me. Change me from the inside out." Say that, and the healing process of wholeness and giftedness is begun. Willingness to admit weakness is the start of wellness.

It's easy to railroad others, and yourself, into seeing your will as paramount to, or surmounting, God's will. It's true: only you get to decide whether the days you have lived thus far bear enlargement.

But enlargement need not mean replication or repetition. You have not lived this day before. God's pleasure is to present each day as newness of life, and that abundantly and above all imagining.

Your life will change when you allow the great force of the Creator to heal you, to lift you up, and free you from the grip of your own tyranny—what you think should be done, how you think it should be done, and when. You see, we can oppress ourselves with the list of "shoulds" that were never designed to heal no matter how well-meaning their intent. We oppress ourselves when we oppress others by "shoulding" all over them. For what we give always comes back to us. God will heal you of all of that. What's more, you can pass on that healing balm to others and keep the healing flow of love passing through you, making you whole each and every day.

Receive the healing balm and be delivered from death into life. If every day begins with the terrifying feeling of, "How many times have I lived this day already?" the healing balm of trust turns that terror into excitation: "This is the first day of the best days of my life."

Resting in God's care and trusting in God's charge, be loved, Beloved. Be loved.

104

THE HONORED GUEST

Mild fawning turns into full-blown fandom, and you're hooked. Imagine you've been preparing a lavish party for your favorite celebrity. You've rented quality table linens, hired a caterer, signed a band, even spent money on flowers and balloons. You've festooned every surface and made sure all was perfect. The honor of this person is evident not just to all who are invited but also to the one who counts the most, your honored guest.

That morning, everything goes haywire. The caterer comes down with the flu. The band cancels the contract. You're sitting around with decorations and linens and nothing else. But just as you start pulling up your guest list to notify everyone of the problems, there's a knock on the door.

You open it, thinking this is the last thing you need right now. Your phone drops from your hand even as your mouth drops open because on your doorstep stands the honored guest! Just as the story is about to tumble out, your guest holds up their hand and says, "Sorry I'm here so early, but I have the day off, and I just thought maybe you could use some help getting ready."

Your favorite celebrity is humble too? This is almost too much to take.

The celebrity isn't kidding. When they say "help" they mean *help*. They put in an order to be picked up at the grocery store, get in the car, and come back ready to cook. Musician friends are called and are happy to come to a party. "Why don't we invite the neighborhood too?" the guest asks. "There's plenty to share and plenty to spare."

Your favorite celebrity is generous too? No wonder you took a shine. What a person! And aren't you brilliant?

Needless to say, your party is far more wonderful than you had ever hoped it could be. The food, made by your guest, is warm and comforting. What you planned to be a formal affair, in deference to who you thought your guest was, becomes a celebration of who your guest is—and who you are—not only for inviting them but also for allowing their humble service.

Everyone eats and is filled. Everyone dances because nobody cares what they look like. The music is upbeat and happy. Everyone takes home leftovers if they want them.

Beloved, God is like the honored guest. We can plan and placate God, try and impress the Creator with our songs, offerings, fancy foods, and our most-wanted guest list. But the truth is, when God arrives and takes on the party, it's a family affair, a neighborhood event, a bash, a blast.

You are more than a place for God to be received, Friend. You are a place God will join and jointer, creating a space of safety and comfort. But it's never an exclusive place, because in God, there is room for everybody. Talk about a party.

Swing wide the door. Invite God to express the divine creativity in you, through you, and with you, for your own welfare and for those around you. It's hard to let go of the ideas we thought we may have wanted for our party, but when we do, things will happen that we didn't know could. Despair will be turned to delight. And sorrow to acceptance and then to joy. Each day we live is a new opportunity to join the table of the honored guest, but it's a table prepared by the guest that proclaims who that guest truly is—a table where you and I, and all of us, are invited to be hosted and be loved, Beloved. Be loved.

105

A NEW STORY BEGINS

Once upon a time you came into the world. The setting of your story was uniquely your own. Perhaps your life story was shared with siblings, perhaps not. Either way, what they experienced and what you experienced weren't perceived in the exact same way.

Your arrival itself proclaimed the news that the Creator not only knew of your existence but made you by hand. Without God, nothing made could have been made. (See John 1:3.) Your presence on this planet is a one-of-a-kind, handmade, original creation. You are a continuation of the original story of humankind, the story of a glorious creature that is part of all God proclaimed, "It is very good." In Hebrew "tov" means good, true, and beautiful.

The good news of the story is this: It's still good. It's still true. It's still beautiful. You're still "tov."

This isn't that story told by some well-meaning folks whereby author-god specializes in writing horror stories, never-ending tales of woe, pain, and suffering, with no homecomings or even rest stops along the way.

The story of God is so much more blessed and bright than endless storms and deepening despair. In God, the story may have rocky climbs, misty valleys, and hard places. None of these are too hard for God. We can rely on our Creator, for we do not know the future. We do not know the end of our story—we cannot—because our story does not end. It keeps going through eternity. You are living but one chapter at a time here.

But there's even more good news, Beloved.

Each step your walk of life takes is never wasted. Every stride can be greater connection with your Creator and deeper union with all that the Creator made and loves. Love is always patient. Infatuation is always in a hurry. The God of true and lasting love is wooing us gently into the life of "tov," and this loving God has eternity to do so.

This place you find yourself isn't the end of your story or anyone else's for that matter. Because your story is my story and the story of all made in the image of God. The story is of God's glory in you, me, and all of us.

Ask God to come to you, Friend, and take over writing your story. Right now, right here, in the midst of your unfinished story. Your life story has yet to completely unfold in real-time. Give the pen back to God, not to circumstances, chance, or people who would tell you your life is meaningless and doesn't matter. Who made them your masters or your ghostwriters? The only author worthy of the authority to write your life story is your loving Creator.

You see, every story has an author, and that author is your authority. Don't turn over authorship to celebrities or billionaires or politicians or consumer culture. Don't turn over authorship to the part of yourself who compares itself to spiritual gurus and the heavy-weights of religion devoid of love. Insisting on solely authoring your own life story, writing the same old lines over and over, is insanity at its most basic. Doing what you think is right in your own eyes without thought for God, others, or yourself, is a horror story in the making.

Turn the page, Beloved! See before you a new chapter with a pristine surface upon which you and God might start something new together. Isn't that exciting! Each day is a new page, you know.

Your story matters to God. You matter to God. You matter to me. You matter to all humanity. You matter to the future. In this time and place, you were made to love and be loved, dear Child of God. This is your story. This is your song. And in the tune of the Great Composer of all songs, in the story of the One who tells all tales, you are loved, Beloved. You are loved.

106

A SONG OF GOD'S FAITHFUL LOVE

Lord, you give me all that I need.
You support me.
You give me my share.
My share is wonderful.
My inheritance is very beautiful.
I praise the Lord because he taught me well.
Even at night he put his instructions deep inside my mind.
I always remember that the Lord is with me.
He is here, close by my side,
so nothing can defeat me.
So my heart and soul will be very happy.
Even my body will live in safety,
because you will not leave me in the place of death.
You will not let your faithful one rot in the grave.
You will teach me the right way to live.
Just being with you will bring complete happiness.
Being at your right side will make me happy forever.

—Psalm 16:5–11 (ERV)

ABOUT THE AUTHORS

Writing partners Leonard Sweet and Lisa Samson have written over one hundred books between them and are excited about this release of the *Sound of Light*. They hope the words that are spoken and heard from within this book are a much needed blessing to all in need.

Leonard Sweet is a prolific author (leonardsweet.com) and professor of semiotics at Drew University, George Fox University, and Northwind Seminary. As a preacher his sermons and ministry resources can be found through Preach the Story (preachthestory.com). He is the publisher at the Salish Sea Press and is also a hospitality proprietor at Sanctuary Seaside (www.sanctuaryseaside.com). He is a social media maven and can be found on Facebook (www.facebook.com/lensweet) and X (x.com/lensweet).

Lisa Samson seeks each day to bring healing, hope, and love to the planet. As a writer, she is a big fan of story and metaphor, seeking out signs, symbols, and songs, to help bring people into closer relationship with God, each other, and the earth. She has three grown children and a son-in-law she absolutely adores, a beloved grandson, and serves as a massage therapist in the Nashville area.

Connect with Len and Lisa as well as other
Sound of Light readers:

Instagram: @be_loved_beloved_be_loved

Facebook: @https://www.facebook.com/people/
The-Sound-of-Light/61560937965593/

Welcome to Our House!

We Have a Special Gift for You

It is our privilege and pleasure to share in your love of Christian books. We are committed to bringing you authors and books that feed, challenge, and enrich your faith.

To show our appreciation, we invite you to sign up to receive a specially selected **Reader Appreciation Gift**, with our compliments. Just go to the Web address at the bottom of this page.

God bless you as you seek a deeper walk with Him!

WE HAVE A GIFT FOR YOU. VISIT:

whpub.me/nonfictionthx

WHITAKER
HOUSE